THE FINAL TESTAMENTS VOL. 6
JESUS CHRIST: THE WAY YET UNKNOWN
(Religion Without Reason – Book 1)

by
Uche Ephraim Chuku

Gotham Books

30 N Gould St.
Ste. 20820, Sheridan, WY 82801
https://gothambooksinc.com/

Phone: 1 (307) 464-7800

© 2025 *Uche Ephraim Chuku*. All rights reserved.

No part of this book may be reproduced, stored in a retrieval system, or transmitted by any means without the written permission of the author.

Published by Gotham Books (May 6, 2025)

ISBN: 979-8-3492-7591-3 (H)
ISBN: 979-8-3492-7589-0 (P)
ISBN: 979-8-3492-7590-6 (E)

Because of the dynamic nature of the Internet, any web addresses or links contained in this book may have changed since publication and may no longer be valid.

The views expressed in this work are solely those of the author and do not necessarily reflect the views of the publisher, and the publisher hereby disclaims any responsibility for them.

CONTENTS

DEDICATION v
ACKNOWLEDGEMENT vi
INTRODUCTION vii
CHAPTER ONE: Historical Origin Of Man's Present World of Darkness.. 1

    The Kingdom And The Outer Darkness............................... 1
    The Father's Glorious Heavenly Kingdom........................... 10
    Graphic Illustration Of Christ's Gospel Of The Kingdom 11
    The Outer Darkness 15
    The Spirits That Sinned And Died.. 18
    The So-Called Kingdoms Of The World.............................. 33
    The Unchanged Will Of The Father For His Fallen Dead Sons In The World.. 50

CHAPTER TWO: The Divine Office Of Jesus Christ Our Messiah 63

    Parable Of The Royal Ship And The Bottomless Dark Ocean 81
    Knowledge Is Inevitable For Salvation 95
    Jesus Christ And The Father Are One; Jehovah/Allah Is One With The World 98
    Jesus Christ As The Only Son Of The Father In The World.. 112
    Jesus Christ As The Only True Light That Enlightens Every Man In The World 123
    Jesus Christ Is Truth And Life.. 127
    Jesus Christ As The Only Way To The Tree Of Life 139
    Jesus Christ, The Interim Paradise And The Ultimate Resurrection 145

Jesus Christ Is The Sole Custodian Of The
Interim Paradise 157
The Ultimate Resurrection 162
CONCLUSION 165
SELECTED BIBLIOGRAPHY 167

DEDICATION

The book is solely dedicated to Jesus Christ of Nazareth, the Divine Incarnation of the Father's miraculous Love and Word of Life for all fallen dead spirits in the world.

ACKNOWLEDGEMENT

My sole gratitude goes to Jesus Christ of Nazareth for the privilege he has granted me to bear this noble cross.

INTRODUCTION

The world is a perilous place. The necessity of spiritual salvation is no longer an unfamiliar field to most human beings on earth. It is also no longer difficult for enlightened minds to appreciate the fact that no human can be able to rekindle or redeem his own captive spirit. That is one of the reasons people arbitrarily turn to customary religions of the world. But customary religions cannot offer genuine spiritual guidance to anyone because they are strictly, worldly institutions. Most of them are overtly misleading.

Most people look up to various kinds of customary religious intercessors for spiritual guidance. But because all customary religions are full-fledged institutions of the world, their so-called religious masters are mere puppets in the hands of the wicked principalities that rule the world. All mystical masters, gurus, sages, buddhas, monks, avatars, and prophets of the world are agents of darkness. They are strictly in business to mislead unenlightened minds, to sustain human ignorance and spiritual enslavement. Relying on such people for spiritual guidance and salvation is completely futile.

Genuine seekers of true spiritual salvation need to be able to correctly distinguish between the true source of spiritual guidance and these misleading agents of darkness. For that, they need to have spiritual insight. But spiritual insight is a divine bequest that can only come from the heavenly Christ. So, genuine seekers of spiritual salvation must first seek to *discover* the true Jesus Christ. Then, they must hold firmly to his true gospel, as he assures that "people who hold on to his teachings will know the truth, and the truth will set them free."

Only a truly transcendent Messiah can be able to extricate captive human spirits from terminal entanglement with matter, and from eternal enslavement to the ruthless principalities of the world. Jesus Christ is that unique personality. He is a heavenly humanitarian. His divine authority and willingness to save have been tried and tested. And he remains ever outstanding in human history.

Only Jesus Christ of Nazareth can provide true spiritual guidance to captive human spirits. Only he can rekindle and lead lost spirits back to their true heavenly origin in Divine Spirit because he is the *only* living spirit in the world. For this reason, the Scripture describes him as "the way, the truth, and the life," and "the resurrection and the life." He is the only true Savior in the world. All other saviors or ways known to humans are false. They can only lead their victims to the impending eternal spiritual death.

Unfortunately, though the name, Jesus Christ, is known all over the world to be synonymous with human salvation, the Divine Essence called "Christ our Savior" has largely remained undiscovered. He personally says in Matt 11:27 that "No one knows the Son except the Father, and no one knows the Father except the Son and any one to whom the Son chooses to reveal him." Most people only rely on misleading notions of his divinity and purpose as propagated by misinformed individuals and covert agents of darkness whose real intent is to distort the truth about him.

Thus, Jesus Christ means different things to different people. The Jews saw him as their own brother but believed that he was a false messiah. They still have not realized that he is indeed the "Christ our Savior." The Romans crucified him, believing that he came to overthrow the great Roman Empire and become King of the whole world. Islamic tradition holds him to be one of the 124,000 prophets sent to the world by Allah. But the Quran even calls him the Messiah. Quran 3:45-46 reads, "O Mary! Lo! Allah giveth thee glad tidings of a word from Him, **whose name is the Messiah**, Jesus, son of Mary, **illustrious in the world and in the**

Hereafter… and **he is of the Righteous**." Yet Muslims regard him as a renegade prophet and a messiah without a definite portfolio.

Customary Christians who consider themselves Jesus's only disciples, believe that he is the true Messiah, the only Savior of the world and the head of their universal Church, yet they worship Jehovah as *God Almighty* in the world. They call Jesus Christ the Prince of Peace but believe that he is son of Jehovah who is the notorious god of war and violence. Customary Christianity simply preaches a false Jesus Christ that is in total harmony with the worldly council of the ruling principalities that is presided over by the notorious Jehovah/Allah.

Adherents of customary Christianity speak of their Church as "One body of Christ," but there are a total of 45,000 different denominations of customary Christianity worldwide, each representing a different type of Christianity with its own beliefs and practices. They each worship and sing praises to Jehovah, God of the world, in the name of Jesus Christ, and that is the worst kind of religious abomination. This is a vivid proof that customary Christianity knows neither the Father nor the true Jesus Christ who's express will is that his true disciples will be "one" in the world. His prayer to the Father before departing the world was, "Holy Father, keep them in thy name, which thou hast given me, **that they may be one, even as we are one**." [John 17:11]

It is obvious therefore, that customary Christianity as presently constituted is antichrist by default. Thus, customary Christianity is, to all intents and purposes, misleading in its understanding of the true nature and mission of Jesus Christ in the world. How can the customary Christian Jesus Christ be able, or even, wish to set anyone free from eternal servitude to the ruling *God Almighty* of the world?

But Jesus Christ already pronounced a disclaimer in advance against multitudes of churchgoers who may consider themselves his disciples merely because they belong to various discordant factions of so-called Christian religion but do not really know him.

"Not everyone who says to me, 'Lord, Lord,' shall enter the kingdom of heaven," he says to such people, "but he who does the will of my Father who is in heaven. On that day [of final the roll call] many will say to me, 'Lord, Lord, did we not prophesy in your name, and cast out demons in your name, and do many mighty works in your name? And then will I declare to them, '**I never knew you**; depart from me, you evildoers." [Matthew 7:21-23]

True Christianity does not exist on earth as a religious group; it is a way of life that exists only in people's hearts. Genuine seekers of true spiritual salvation will need to search diligently within themselves to ***discover*** the true Jesus Christ that saves. And when they find him, he will not be one mysterious *voice from heaven* that a human being can hear with his ears. He will not be the kind of *harsh scotching light* that blinded Saul of Tarsus on his way to Damascus. And he will not be the mystical Jesus Christ whose dossier was magically downloaded on Paul in a three-year intense mystical tutorial in the desert of Arabia.

Certainly, the true Jesus Christ will not be the overwhelming intense luminosity that people with Near-death experience (NDE) routinely see at the end of a very long dark tunnel. Neither will he be the one that is in league with the unforgiving Jehovah, god of Israel, and the menacing, so-called archangels of this world.

People who genuinely seek true spiritual salvation in the name of Jesus Christ of Nazareth must hold on to his exact words. They must be bold and courageous. And they can start by reexamining the known attributes of Jesus Christ and Jehovah/Allah critically and objectively. For instance, Jesus Christ stands for peace, and he is appropriately called the Prince of Peace. But Jehovah/Allah is well-known to be notoriously violent and highhanded, and he is universally recognized as the God of war. Clearly Jesus Christ and Jehovah/Allah do not share the same qualities, purpose, and mannerism.

In any case, Jesus Christ gives a perfect rule of the thumb for the compatibility test. He says, "Either make the tree good, and its fruits good; or make the tree bad, and its fruits bad; for the tree is known by its fruit." [Matthew 12:33] He assures that he and his Father are "one," meaning that they share the same will and purpose and are perfectly united in their actions and goal. "Truly, truly, I say to you," he says, "the Son can do nothing of his own accord, but only what he sees the Father doing; for whatever he does, that the Son does likewise. ... For as the Father raises the dead and gives them life, so also the Son gives life to whom he will. [John 5:19-21]

Jesus Christ: The Way Yet Unknown tells the story of the true Jesus Christ right from its beginning, clarifying his true divine personality and his mission in the world. He is the author of humankinds' spiritual evolution, which started with Adam and Eve far back in Eden. He *first* appeared to Adam and Eve in Eden as the heavenly Spirit of Knowledge, and during his *second coming*, he purposely manifested as the Father's Incarnate Word of Life among Adam's descendants. Jesus Christ was the same heavenly Spirit of Knowledge that promised eternal life to Adam and Eve and assured them that he would eventually return to bear witness to the deliberately falsified events of Eden.

For obvious reasons, Jehovah maliciously truncated the history of Jesus Christ as the Father's Incarnate World of Life, making it seem as if humankind's spiritual evolution started with Abraham and not with Adam and Eve. That is why it has been practically impossible for most people to understand the true nature and mission of Jesus Christ in the world.

Jehovah so confused even the Jews that they simply regarded Jesus Christ as a son of David, or son of Abraham, a mere prophet and even a false messiah. Jesus Christ tried to reason with them but was unsuccessful. "Why is it," he asked them, "that the Messiah is said to be the son of David? ... "Since David called the Messiah 'Lord,' how can the Messiah be his son?" [Luke 20:41-44(NLT)] He also said to them, "Truly, truly, I say to you, before Abraham was, I am." [Jn 8:58] But none of them understood him because Jehovah had thoroughly indoctrinated them all with falsehood.

Of course, the heavenly Christ did not suddenly emerge on earth from nowhere and became the Son of man. His *second coming* in human form was sequel to his *first coming* in his spiritual nature. The Scripture reveals explicit links between his first and second coming, the most important being his solemn enduring promise to grant eternal life to captive human spirits. As the heavenly Spirit of Knowledge, the heavenly Christ assured that **"man will not surely die"** as Jehovah, God of Eden, had threatened. He promised to lead Adam and his posterity to the forbidden Tree of Eternal Life.

In the appointed time, the Father's Word of Life "became human and made his home among us. He was full of unfailing love and faithfulness. And we have [all] seen his glory, the glory of the Father's one and only Son." [John 1:14(NLT)] So, as the Father's Incarnate Word of Life, Jesus Christ continues to reiterate the same promise of eternal life to humankind. "I am the resurrection and the life," he assures. "Anyone who believes in me will live, even after dying. Everyone who lives in me and believes in me will never ever die." [John 11:25-26(NLT)]

Thus, we must begin the journey of discovery of the true Jesus Christ from the very beginning. He is the only Savior of captive human spirits, the only true *Way* to the Divine Tree of eternal life. So, he says to all genuine seekers of spiritual salvation, "And this is eternal life, that they know thee the only true Father, and [the true] Jesus Christ whom thou hast sent." [John 17:3]

CHAPTER ONE

HISTORICAL ORIGIN OF MAN'S PRESENT WORLD OF DARKNESS

THE KINGDOM AND THE OUTER DARKNESS

The Scripture says that "The world is a dark place, and its people have no light." [2 Esdras 14:20 (GNB)] This statement of fact captures the intrinsic nature of the universe that grew out of total darkness of the primordial Outer Darkness. It reinforces the fact that darkness overwhelms the entire universe, that all forms of universal luminosity are false lights. So, darkness does not only mean absence of artificial light of stars and man-made light sources, but it also includes inner gloominess, which manifests as various forms of evilness in all worldly beings. All forms of human vices stem from inner darkness—falsehood, selfishness, pride, arrogance, immorality, envy, jealousy, treachery, hostility, outburst of anger, vengeance, bloodshed, and others. These apply equally to Jehovah/Allah and the so-called gods of the world.

Darkness also means lack of knowledge and falsehood. People of the world lack knowledge, and they live in falsehood. Jehovah/Allah epitomizes falsehood because he is the acclaimed God of the world. In fact, Jesus Christ says that Jehovah/Allah "was a murderer from the beginning, and has nothing to do with the truth, because there is no truth in him. When he lies, he speaks according to his own nature, for he is a liar and the father of lies." [John 8:44]

The central theme of Christ's mission in the world is "to reveal the truth." He came to reveal the Father and his true spiritual Kingdom to ignorant humans who erroneously see and worship Jehovah/Allah as *God Almighty* in the world. Thus, he says, "For this I was born, and for this I have come into the world, to bear witness to the truth." [John 18:37

Indeed, a person who walks in darkness is lost. He will not know where he is or where he is going. He will not be able to distinguish between what is good and what is evil, or between his true friend and archenemy. In addition, a man in darkness can "believe" anything he hears. To him, any voice that speaks out of his darkness can easily become whatever he claims to be. Therefore, true light is the truth that Jesus Christ reveals to the people that dwell in this world of darkness.

The Scripture says that Jesus Christ is "the true light that enlightens every man [in the world]" [John 1:9] He "came as light into the world, that whoever believes in [him] may not remain in darkness." [John 12:46] Everyone knows that light is good, and anyone that is trapped in darkness naturally yearns for light or for the true way out of darkness. He yearns to come to terms with basic reality. Jesus Christ is reality. Hence the Scripture says, regarding his sudden advent into the world, "The people who walked in darkness have seen a great light; those who dwelt in a land of deep darkness, on them has light shined." [Isaiah 9:2]

This scriptural verse suggests a sudden emergence of great joy among the people who dwell in the land of deep darkness. Indeed, it is natural to expect that people caught up in a region of pitch darkness would rejoice at the sudden influx of light, and that they would gladly abandon all the shady ways of darkness. That has not been the case at all in the human situation. Although "the light has come into the world, men [continued to] loved darkness rather than light, because their deeds were evil."[John 3:19]

Surely, something sinister is amiss in the human situation. Falsehood has become so deeply ingrained into the human psyche. Religion and other indoctrinating agencies of the world work tirelessly to sustain the inner darkness in people. As a result, people generally prefer falsehood to the truth. As the scripture says, "No one after drinking old wine desires new; for he says, 'The old is good.'" [Luke 5:39] Thus, humans who have long walked in darkness, prefer the ways of darkness rather than gladly and wholeheartedly embracing the true light of the heavenly Christ. Rather than embracing the light of truth that guarantees blissful eternal life to their captive spirits, people willfully choose eternal spiritual death in the Outer Darkness.

Jesus Christ came as the light of truth into the world that we may become thoroughly informed. He came that we may objectively reexamine all that we had heard and believed about Jehovah/Allah, the god of Eden. The Messiah came that we may know exactly where we are, and that we may knowingly choose the perfect spiritual Kingdom of the Father over our present world of darkness. The true light is here to reveal our true heavenly Father, so that we may clearly distinguish between him and Jehovah/Allah who rules this present world of darkness.

Since the inception of the world, ignorant humans have seen no other form and heard no other voice but those of Jehovah/Allah, claiming to be the only God in existence. "I am Jehovah, and there is no other, besides me there is no God," he says. [Isaiah 45:5] Ignorant humans whole-heartedly believed his insinuations of absolute sovereignty, because they knew no other standard by which to scrutinize his claims. Hence, he remained undisputed *God* to all the people that walked in darkness.

But is Jehovah/Allah really the Father that Jesus Christ reveals to the world? Is he really the Father who dwells in unsearchable light? Is Jehovah/Allah's fallen dead spirit really the source of perfect heavenly existence? Is the Father who is eternal Light really the inventor of this world of darkness? Are the imperfect *heavens* of this overwhelming darkness really the proper abode of perfect spirits? And should right-thinking human beings not rightly expect the Father's perfect spiritual Kingdom to transcend the entire dark universe? What is the truth?

The spiritual journey of our captive dead spirits back to the Blessed Tree of Life is the journey of discovery. We need to discover and distinguish the Father from Jehovah/Allah who is but an imposter. Jesus Christ calls this ultimate discovery eternal life itself. "This is eternal life," he says, "that they [beguiled human beings] know thee the only true Father, and Jesus Christ whom thou hast sent." [John 17:3]

Jesus Christ made it clear that Jehovah/Allah is neither his Father nor the Tree of Life that our fallen dead spirits earnestly yearn for. He says, "You search the scriptures [of the dark world], because you think that in them you have eternal life; ... yet you refuse to come to me [the divine light of truth] that you may have life." This is because "You know neither me nor my Father;" he says, "if you knew me, you would know my Father also. ... [but] **His voice you have never heard, his form you have never seen**; and you do not have his word abiding in you,... [So,] "No one knows the Son except the Father, and **no one knows the Father except the Son and any one to whom the Son chooses to reveal him**. [John 5:37-40; 8:19; Matthew 11:27]

The Jewish religious authorities persecuted and murdered Jesus the Son of man because they were convinced that he was not the Son of Jehovah, their god. They were sure that Jehovah did not send him into the world. Of course, the fact that Jesus Christ was "**sent into the world**" clearly implies that he and the Father who sent him did not belong to the world. The Father and his perfect heavenly abode transcend the entire material universe and its gods.

Top Jewish religious authorities testified to these facts. "This man is not from Jehovah," they affirmed, "for he does not keep the sabbath... we know that this man is a sinner. ... we are disciples of [Jehovah, god of] Moses. We know that Jehovah has spoken to Moses, but as for this man, **we do not know where he comes from**." [John 9:16, 24, 28-29]

These were well-substantiated testimonies, from men who knew Jehovah very well. It was only obvious that if the top Jewish religious authorities did not know where Jesus Christ came from, they did not also know his Father who sent him. Sadly, customary

Christians, believing that they now know better than the Jews did, now declare that Jehovah is the Father of Jesus Christ.

However, even the very Apostles of Jesus Christ had great problem understanding whom he referred to as his Father. They did not also know exactly where he came from, or the difference between the Father's perfect spiritual Kingdom and the mystical kingdoms of the world. Apostle **Thomas** had declared, "Lord, we do not know where you [came from or where you] are going; how can we know the way?" Apostle **Philip** was convinced that the Father was not Jehovah, god of the Jews, so he instinctively demanded clarification from the Messiah. "Lord, show us the Father, and we shall be satisfied." [John 14:5, 8]

Jesus Christ answered their probing questions by practically exemplifying the Father's eternal character amongst them. He told them plainly that he and his Father share the same perfect attributes. But they still did not understand because the information was beyond their mental imagination at the time. They remained greatly troubled because they had known no other *God* except Jehovah and had heard of no other Heaven except Jehovah's mystical heavens of this world. Then, Jesus Christ told them in a very subtle way that he and his Father are one. "If you had known me, you would have known my Father also; henceforth you know him and have seen him," he said to them. [John 14:7]

Some Jewish followers of Jesus Christ believed that he was just a great prophet. Some called him son of David and others believed he was the reincarnation of "John the Baptist, Elijah, Jeremiah, or one of the prophets." [Matthew 16:14] But the Father testified of his Son to them through the mouth of Apostle Simon Peter, who spontaneously responded to the Messiah's question about his true nature. Jesus Christ had asked his own Apostles, "But who do you say that I am?" And Peter said, "You are the Christ, **the Son of *the living* God**." [Matthew 16:13-16]

The significance of Peter's strong testimony lies in the fact that Jesus Christ was not just the Son of *God*, but actually "**the**

only Son of *the Living God*" in this nether world. Peter's testimony gave perspective to the Apostle's understanding of Christ's consistent utterances and works of true love. It helped them to understand clearly that the Father of Jesus Christ was certainly not Jehovah whom the Jews had always known. The Father is "the Living Divine Spirit," while Jehovah, God of the Jews, is merely a fallen dead spirit.

Both the Bible and the Quran collaborate on the fact that Jehovah/Allah is not the Father of Jesus Christ. Jehovah himself says in Isaiah 42:8; 43:11, "I am Jehovah, that is my name; **my glory I give to no other**, ... "I, I am Jehovah, and **besides me there is no savior**." And Quran 25:2; 5:73 say, "He unto whom belongeth the sovereignty of the heavens and the earth [of the world], he hath chosen no son **nor hath he any [Christ-like] partner in the sovereignty** [of his worldly domain]. ... "They surely disbelieve who say: Lo! Allah is the third of three; when there is no God save the One God [Allah]."

Thus, Jehovah/Allah does not even belong to the fictitious *Holy Trinity* of customary Christianity. And since both the Bible and the Quran claim that Jehovah/Allah created the human world alone, it means that neither the Father nor Jesus Christ has a hand in the imperfect contraption. Customary Christians find this aspect of the gospel truth very hard to accept even though the scriptures make that explicit. In fact, the Bible admonishes true Christ-followers saying, "Do not love the world or the things in the world. If anyone loves the world, love for the Father is not in him. **For all that is in the world, ... is not of the Father** but is of the world [and its gods]." [1 John 2:15-16]

The Quran on its part, describes Jesus Christ as belonging to the "Righteous" Father who transcends the world, while also acknowledging that he is illustrious both in the world and in the perfect heavenly abode of the Father. "The Messiah, Jesus, son of Mary, [is] **illustrious in the world and in the Hereafter**," says

Quran 3:45,... and he is of the Righteous [Father of the Hereafter]."

Human beings never knew about the true *Hereafter* till Jesus Christ appeared and spoke about the heavenly Kingdom of the Father and about heavenly exodus for the sons of the resurrection. Jehovah/Allah only promises a refurbished world order, a refurbished *New* Jerusalem to his ignorant followers because he is earthbound and has no access to the real Hereafter.

Human beings never knew the Father because they were not his creation. Humans are one of the numerous organic lifeforms that evolved naturally on planet Earth as encoded in the primordial universal blueprint. Captive human spirits belong to the family of fallen dead spirits that violated the heavenly norm of perfection and were spewed out of the heavenly Kingdom of the Father. They are born in darkness, and they need to be spiritually reborn. Jesus Christ says, "Truly, truly, I say to you, unless one is born anew, he cannot see the kingdom of the Father." [John 3:3] They must be "reborn—not with a physical birth resulting from human passion or plan, but a birth that comes from the Father."[John 1:13(NLT)]

Jesus Christ came to rekindle and lead captive human spirits to their true origin in the Father. The Father is the true Source of eternal life that dead human spirits earnestly yearn for. He is the symbolic Blessed Tree of Life, mentioned in the ill-fated story of Eden. Jehovah/Allah forbade knowledge of the Father for humans, for obvious reasons. He intended to impersonate the Father in the world, so he willfully kept human beings in the dark. He threatened that human beings would die if they ever sought the knowledge of the difference between him and the Father. "You may freely eat of every tree of the garden;" he decreed, "but of the tree of the knowledge of good and evil you shall not eat, for **in the day that you eat of it you shall die.**" [Genesis 2:16-17]

Jehovah/Allah lied, and that was consistent with his innate nature. He knew that if human beings re-discovered the Father, they would realize that he had been nothing but an impostor. He knew that captive human spirits would regain true eternal spiritual life if they reached the Blessed Tree of Life. And knowing that he was already destined for eternal perdition at the close of the Father's period of grace by his own personal choice, he schemed to drag ignorant human spirits along with him.

He invested all his energy in Eden toward sustaining human ignorance. And when that failed, he placed all sorts of physical and mystical obstacles on the way to the Blessed Tree of Life. The Scripture says that "He put living creatures [his occult operatives] and a flaming sword which turned in all directions at the east side of the garden. **This was to keep anyone from coming near [the Father who is] the tree that gives life.**" [Genesis 3:24 (GNB)]

Indeed, Jehovah/Allah has managed to sustain human ignorance since his defeat in Eden. He has managed to obscure knowledge of the Father by posing as God Almighty to religious believers. But the true light that enlightens every man is increasingly revealing the Father to many in the world, making them realize that Jehovah/Allah is just an impostor. Jehovah/Allah's best of schemes will ultimately come to naught in the end. Even now, he is increasingly becoming frustrated, desperate and suicidal.

Needless to stress that a God who fights a battle he knows he can never win is in a worse state of ignorance than human beings. Jehovah/Allah may have succeeded in delaying the truth, but he cannot suppress the truth forever. Jesus Christ assures that "nothing is hid that shall not be made manifest, nor anything secret that shall not be known and come to light." [Luke 8:17] He also assures that his true "gospel of the kingdom will be preached throughout the whole world, as a testimony to all nations; [before] the end will come." [Matthew 24:14]

Jehovah/Allah, with his horde of occult and human militia cannot stop the true gospel of Jesus Christ. The Father will ultimately stand out in the world as the Blessed Tree of Life, and Jesus Christ will resurrect all genuine seekers of spiritual rebirth on the last day. "For this is the will of my Father," he says, "that everyone who sees the Son and believes in him should have eternal life; and I will raise him up at the last day." [John 6:40]

The duty of *The Final Testaments* is to highlight the difference between the Father and Jehovah/Allah, between the Father's perfect spiritual Kingdom and the false kingdoms of the world of darkness, and between the true spiritual life eternal and the false life of the world. The Father is eternal, infinite Divine Spirit. His heavenly Kingdom is the perfect abode of living spirits. The kingdoms of the world, on the other hand, are the joint enterprise of the heavenly dropouts. Living spirits are sons of Light, while all fallen dead spirits in the world are sons of darkness.

The book of Revelation cryptically alludes to Jehovah/Allah and the so-called archangels as rulers of humans' world. And though they pose as *living* spirits to ignorant humans, they are equally fallen dead spirits, like every organic lifeform in the world. Revelation 12:3(GNB) says, "There was **a huge red dragon with seven heads** and … a crown on each of his heads." And Revelation 17:11 (GNB) adds that Jehovah/Allah, "the beast that was once [spiritually] alive, but lives no longer, is itself **an eighth king** who is **one of the seven [other kings** that rule the kingdoms of men]." These notorious eight, together form "**the principalities**, the powers, the world rulers of this present darkness and the *mystical* hosts of wickedness in the *hidden* places," which are alluded to in Ephesians 6:12.

In fact, principalities refer to territories or jurisdictions of princes, not of kings. Therefore, though Jehovah/Allah and his faceless partners in crime claim the title of "kings" in the world, they are but fallen dead sons or "princes." They are no longer worthy even to be called sons of the Father who is the eternal King over entire existence. The Father's perfect spiritual Kingdom is the only true one that exists. No true kingdom exists in the entire universe, which is just a grand Sheol and a place of false existence.

THE FATHER'S GLORIOUS HEAVENLY KINGDOM

The diagram below gives a graphic explanation of Christ's gospel of the true Kingdom. It is a very simple schematic representation of the complex spiritual information that is contained in the true gospel of Jesus Christ. As an engineer, I know the importance of sketches and diagrams. They convey good visual illustrations of human imagination. The diagram captures the two distinct eternal realms of Light and Darkness that make up Ultimate Reality and shows the unbridgeable chasm that exists between them. Anyone who understands the diagram has essentially grasped the central message of Christ's gospel of redemption.

Some people think that the diagram is an occult symbol and that I belong to some secret society. But it has nothing whatsoever to do with occultism, and I belong to no mystical or esoteric order of any sort. I am just an honest human being, representing the average genuine seekers of true spiritual salvation, and expressing what we all feel and can understand as human beings.

Jesus Christ came for ordinary human beings on the earth. He picked fishermen and the common people in the society and made them apostles of his heavenly mission. He told them the truth about the Father, his perfect heavenly Kingdom and his gracious offer of spiritual redemption. They understood him clearly, accepted the Father's gracious offer, and received their spiritual salvation.

Jesus Christ also picked me up as an ordinary seafarer who knew close to nothing about his real divine nature and mission in the world. Then, he revealed and continued to reveal to me profound information about myself, about himself, about our true heavenly Father and his gracious offer of spiritual resurrection. He also opened my eyes to a clearer understanding of universal darkness, as it applies to false light, false life, false Gods, and false existence. Thus, everything about Jehovah/Allah and his colonial

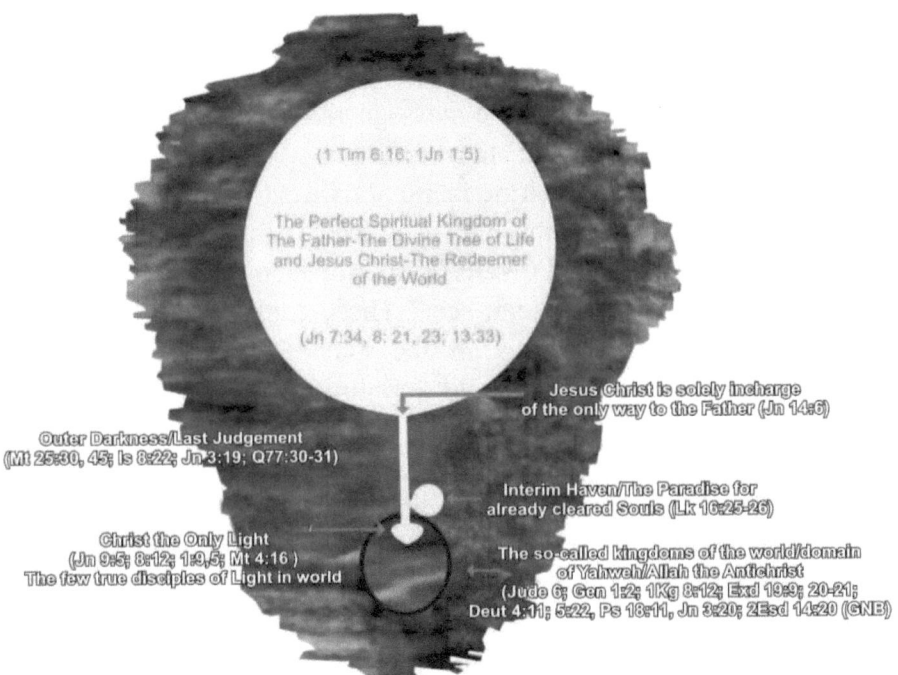

claims over the human world stands out as a counterfeit of true heavenly ideals.

GRAPHIC ILLUSTRATION OF CHRIST'S GOSPEL OF THE KINGDOM

The big bright sphere represents the spiritual realm of Divine Light, which is the Father's heavenly Kingdom. The surrounding dark region, on the other hand, represents the physical realm of Darkness, which Jesus Christ also called the Outer Darkness. Of course, one cannot possibly put a definite hedge around the Father's eternal, infinite spiritual Kingdom, or around the eternal, infinite expanse of the Outer Darkness. The diagram only serves to simplify the complex spiritual essence of the truth to bring it within the limits of human comprehension.

The Scripture is explicit about the fact that the Father is Divine Light and that there is no darkness in him or within his heavenly abode whatsoever. "This is the message we have heard from him [Jesus Christ] and proclaim to you," says 1 John 1:5, "that **the Father is Light** and **in him is no darkness at all**." Then, 1 Timothy 6:16 describes the Father as the Supreme Being "Who alone has immortality and **dwells in unapproachable light**, whom no man has ever seen or can see." These cannot be said about Jehovah/Allah who belongs in the Outer Darkness and has personally "said that he would [continue to] dwell in thick darkness." [1 Kings 8:12]

No human being can see or hear the voice of the Father because the Father is perfect Spirit, and he dwells beyond the limits of human experiences, both physical and mystical. Human beings never knew the Father because they were not his creation. Humans did not fall from heaven because they were never in heaven. They were never sons of the heavenly Kingdom, but organic mutants generated by heavenly dropouts within the Outer Darkness to serve as motorized mortal cloaks for their dead spirits. In fact, all *living* beings outside the Father's heavenly Kingdom are spiritually dead entities. "I tell you this, brethren:" says 1 Corinthians 15:50, "flesh and blood cannot inherit the kingdom of the Father, nor does the perishable inherit the imperishable."

Jehovah/Allah refers to himself as "the *first and the last*" among humans on earth, meaning he is the *first* among all fallen dead sons of the Father on earth. According to 1 Kings 8:12, he dwells permanently in thick darkness within the Outer Darkness, and he rules over ignorant men and women who are equally dead entities. Even though he poses as *God Almighty* to ignorant humans and expects people to believe that he is the Father "who dwells in unapproachable light," the Scripture expressly says that "he made darkness his covering around him," as a matter of inevitability. [Psalms 18:11] He did not even attempt to disguise that fact when he personally led the Israelites through their ill-fated Exodus. On one occasion, "the people [of Israel] stood afar off, while Moses drew near to the thick darkness where Jehovah was." [Exodus 20:21]

The **realm of "unapproachable light,"** is the eternal spiritual realm of perfection. This is the *proper* abode of the Father, the Christ and all living spirits who are good sons of the Father. In the Father's glorious Kingdom, there is absolute light, eternal life and absolute bliss. There is perfect love and harmony between the Father and all his sons. According to the Gnostics, our true heavenly Father is "depth and silence, beyond any name or predicate [ever known to human beings], the absolute, the source of good spirits who together form the *Pleroma* or **realm of Light**."

In the Gnostic tradition, the *Pleroma* means the state of total fullness of the realm of Divine Light, the totality and harmony of divine powers and emanations of the Father. These do not apply to the imperfect universe or any of its false kingdoms that exist outside the Father's realm of perfection.

The Father is the Supreme Source of all spirits in existence. All perfect spirits dwell within the sphere of the Father's positive influence in the realm of "unapproachable light." They are sons of Light. Jesus Christ says, "There is more than enough room in my Father's home" for all the spirits that live by the heavenly norm of perfection. [John 14:2(NLT)] So, all spirits in our material universe are corrupted, fallen and dead to their divine privileges in Divine Spirit. Spewed out of the *Pleroma* or the heavenly household of the Father, they now subsist in the Outer Darkness, within the sphere of the Father's negative influence. They are now sons of Darkness.

Jehovah/Allah, the so-called archangels and gods of the world, humans and other organic beings in the world are corrupted spirits. They do not belong to the "realm of unapproachable light," but are eternally confined in the Outer Darkness because their deeds are evil. All corrupted spirits in the universe are sinners.

They are all hostile, proud, dishonest, self-seeking, envious, and they are permanently scheming evil.

Jesus Christ alludes to the eternal chasm that exists between the Father's glorious heavenly Kingdom and our present world of darkness in so many ways. He says to all inhabitants of the world, "You are from [the Outer Darkness] below, I am from [the Father's heavenly Kingdom] above; **you are of this world [of darkness], I am not of this world**. ... "Little children, yet a little while I am with you. You will seek me; and as I said to the Jews so now I say to you, '**Where I am going you cannot come**.'" [John 8:23; 13:33] Then, he makes it explicit that he is the only *way*, the only *bridge* through that chasm for every genuine seeker of spiritual redemption. "I am the way, the truth, and the life," he says, "No one can come to the Father except through me." [John 14:6(NLT)]

Next, Jesus Christ declares his divine mission in the world, outlines the process of redemption, and counsels every genuine seeker of spiritual rebirth on what to do. "I have come as light into the world, that whoever believes in me may not remain in [the Outer] Darkness," he says. Then, he added, "Truly, truly, I say to you, **unless one** [from the world of darkness] **is born anew, he cannot see the Kingdom of the Father**." So, "While you have the light," he counsels, "believe in the light, **that you may become sons of Light**." [John 12:46; 3:3; 12:36]

Here, being "born anew" further stresses the fact that man's present worldly birth, life and ethics directly contradict those of the Father's heavenly Kingdom. To qualify to regain true life in the Father's perfect spiritual Kingdom, captive human spirits must knowingly wean themselves of all aspects of their present nature that belong to the outer darkness. They must knowingly confront and overcome Jehovah/Allah and all his evil works. They must denounce the world of darkness in its entirety.

To that effect, the Scripture counsels all true seekers of the heavenly life, saying, "Do not be conformed to this world [of darkness] but be transformed by the renewal of your mind, that you may prove what is the will of the Father, what is good and acceptable and perfect [for the heavenly life]. [Romans 12:2]

Titus 3:3-7 says, "For **we ourselves were once foolish** [in revolting against perfection], disobedient, led astray, slaves to various passions and pleasures, passing our days in malice and envy, hated by men and hating one another; but when the goodness and loving kindness of the Father our Savior appeared, he saved us, not because of deeds done by us in righteousness, but in virtue of his own mercy, **by the washing of regeneration and renewal in the Holy Spirit**, which **he poured out upon us richly through Jesus Christ our Savior**, so **that we might** be justified by his grace and **become heirs in hope of eternal life**."

Thus, the Scripture says to all genuine seekers of ultimate spiritual rebirth, "Take no part in the unfruitful works of darkness, but instead expose them." [Ephesians 5:11] Writing *The Final Testaments* is my own practical way of abiding by that wise counsel.

THE OUTER DARKNESS

Beyond the Father's infinite realm of perfect Light is the infinite realm of total Darkness, which Jesus Christ simply calls the "Outer Darkness." These two eternal realms exist as extreme aspects of the Father who is the Infinite Source of entire existence. The two infinite arenas are eternally demarcated in the Father's eternal divine masterplan. The realm of perfect Light represents the sphere of the Father's positive influence, while the opposite realm of perfect Darkness is the sphere of his negative effects. While the realm of perfect Light is spiritual and destined for eternal life and perfect divine activities, the realm of perfect Darkness is lifeless and serves as serene repository of all material aspects of existence.

Since the Father is Light and Light is Life and Life means activities, the Outer Darkness is naturally lifeless by divine design because it was devoid of divine Light. The Outer Darkness is a spiritual *void*, meaning it is a perfectly endowed material arena in absolute state of tranquility. It can be likened to a perfect nature reserve without any living being or activity in it. As we can see therefore, the realm of Darkness is perfect for its divine purpose. It is the fallen dead spirits and their corrupted activities within the outer darkness that are evil and imperfect.

The Scripture reiterates that "the angels that **did not keep their original position** [of perfection in the Father's heavenly Kingdom] but **forsook their own proper dwelling place** he has reserved with eternal bonds **under dense darkness** [in the Outer Darkness] for the judgment of the great day." [Jude 6 (NWT)] The fallen sons of light eventually set up the finite howling universe as an alternative dwelling place within the Outer Darkness where they now live and die and gnash their teeth.

Activities of the truly *living* spirits uphold perfect order in the realm of Light, but the fallen spirits cannot possibly establish real order in their prison of darkness because they are but *dead* spirits. And even with the artificial lights of the stars and man-made light sources, the universe will forever remain a dark place, a spiritual *void*, and a lifeless arena. Our makeshift finite universe will remain chaotic, imperfect and irredeemable forever.

The Scripture says that the fallen spirits were groping hopelessly in total darkness in the Outer Darkness before their cataclysmic *big bang* that brought about the chaotic universal mushroom, false light of stars, animated lifeforms and false existence. "In the beginning," says Genesis 1:1-2(TEV), "when *Elohim* [the fallen spirits] created the universe, the earth was formless and desolate. The raging ocean that covered everything was engulfed in **total darkness**, and the power of *Elohim* [the fallen spirits] was moving over the water."

For spirits that had basked in eternal glory of divine light in the Father's glorious Kingdom, becoming suddenly engulfed in total darkness meant total incapacitation and eternal self-damnation. And since divine life and activities depend entirely on true light and they no longer have that, the groping spirits were indeed spiritually dead. They needed any kind of light before they could even begin to grapple with other eternal impediments that confronted them as fallen dead spirits.

The Genesis account of the creation of the universe captures the groping spirits desperately crying out for light. "Let there be light" was their collective outcry against total darkness. The *big bang* became the outcome of their collective outburst. The *big bang* was an unexpected breakthrough, but it represented an epic triumph over total darkness for the fallen dead spirits. Nevertheless, the *big bang* was only a captured moment of space-time continuum. That meant that the expanding universal mushroom was restricted in space and time within the eternal infinite expanse of the Outer Darkness.

But despite the presence of artificial light of stars that enables organic existence within the universal mushroom, it remains a prison of darkness for the corrupted spirits because they have eternally fallen short of divine glory of the Father. Organic existence within finite space represents *false living* and it involves acute limitations. Limitations bring about selfishness, greed, opportunism, power mongering, bitter rivalry, ungodliness, conceit, betrayal, rancor, willful oppression and much more. Therefore, anarchy reigns supremely in the universe because true light, life and love do not and can never exist in the realm of darkness. Here, evilness overshadows goodness, the mighty dominates the weak, and the winner simply takes it all without feeling any remorse whatsoever.

This is the background of Jehovah/Allah's colonial dominion over ignorant humans on planet Earth. Jehovah/Allah and the so-called archangels that rule the kingdoms of men are wicked spirits and sheer opportunists. They made themselves kings, lords and gods and heartlessly lord it over their less informed kith and kin, turning them into religious slaves. But, they are false kings, lords and gods, because the only true Kingdom in existence remains the Father's glorious domain above. According to Jehovah/Allah himself "there is no peace for the wicked," in the Fatherless kingdoms of the world. Thus, both those that dominate and oppress others and those that are dominated and oppressed in the world are equally distressed and unhappy.

THE SPIRITS THAT SINNED AND DIED

"The spirit that sins shall die." So says Ezekiel 18:20. This simple statement represents the eternal norm of perfection, and the actual genesis of our present world of darkness was rooted in its violation.

Clearly, this divine precept does not refer to sinful men and women or to the imperfect material worlds of mortal beings. Humans are born in sin, and they live and die in sin. Men and women that sin rather prosper and live longer in the world of darkness that Jehovah/Allah rules. It is an undeniable fact that Jehovah/Allah himself protects and favors evil men and women who serve his devilish interest in the world. "Because they work for me," says Jehovah. [Ezekiel 29:20] Thus, Isaiah 13:5, speaking about the ruthless army that Jehovah was assembling "to destroy the whole earth," refers to them as "Jehovah and the weapons of his indignation."

"The spirit that sins shall die," is the eternal norm governing the life of perfect spirits within the perfect spiritual Kingdom of the Father. Every living spirit within the Father's realm of perfection understands this divine precept as the basic principle of perfection, and as a standard reaffirmation of every spirit's **natural freewill**. This simple statement shows clearly that even perfection is not without a price. For instance, if perfection means a spirit dwelling in the realm of Light and always behaving in a specific manner, then any slight deviation from that *proper* pattern automatically renders the spirit imperfect. If perfection means absolute goodness, then the perfect spirit must not give in to any iota of wickedness, in any form or manner.

Speaking of this in a different way, perfection is like a ship crew standing on the deck of a ship floating upon a deep dark ocean. For as long as he continues to stand and perform his statutory duties within his *proper* bounds on the deck, he is safe and happy **onboard**. Any second he steps off the ship's deck for any reason whatsoever, **he drowns** in the deep dark ocean, unavoidably.

Just as the ship crew standing on the deck of the ship is never in any doubt that taking a single step in the wrong direction would cause him to drown in the deep dark ocean, perfect spirits in the heavenly household of the Father have no doubt about what actions are right or wrong for them. They have no doubt that acting contrary to the heavenly norm will lead to eternal death in the Outer Darkness. So, it is within their divine freewill to constantly choose between right and wrong to continue to live in perfection or to die eternal spiritual death in the Outer Darkness.

Needless to stress that the same fate confronts whosoever steps off the safe limit on a ship floating upon a deep dark ocean, whether he is the captain of the ship or the lowest ranking crew member. It goes to say therefore, that the divine norm of perfection eternally applies equally to the Father as it does to his innumerable perfect sons because there is only one standard of perfection in the Father's glorious Kingdom. Perfection is forever perfect! The Father does not have a different standard of goodness for his own perfection and another standard for the harmonious spirits that emanated from him, for as long as they continue to dwell in the same domain.

Hence, the Scripture admonishes, "Let no one say when he is tempted, 'I am tempted by the Father'; for **the Father cannot be tempted with evil** and he himself tempts no one." [James 1:13] The Father cannot be tempted to do evil, neither can any truly *living* spirit. That is what perfection is all about.

Jesus Christ has been called the only true Son of our perfect Father in the world because he descended into the sinful world as a truly *living* spirit. He bears the eternal insignia of the heavenly norm of perfection and is in absolute harmony with the Father's divine will. He practically exemplified this norm in the world when he sympathized with, and prayed for the people who persecuted, whipped, and nailed him on the tree rather than get angry with them.

Surely, Jesus Christ had the power and very good reasons to have violently restrained his human and occult assailants on earth, but he rather prayed for the Father's forgiveness and mercy upon them. Thus, he practically proved that, as the only true Son of the living Father in the world, '**he could not be tempted to do anything evil**,' even in this sinful world. "Father, forgive them;" he prayed, "for they know not what they do." [Luke 23:34]

Unconditional love for all was the personal attitude of Jesus Christ toward all his "enemies" in the world. That was perfectly in line with what he taught and continues to teach entire humankind even to this day. He could justifiably tell human beings to love one another as he loved us all. He said and still says to us, "I say to you, Love your enemies and pray for those who persecute you, **so that you may be sons of your Father who is in heaven**,... You, therefore, must be perfect, as your heavenly Father is perfect." [Matthew 5:44, 48]

Evidently, the divine norm of perfection does not concern Jehovah/Allah who is easily provoked by every innocent action or inaction of human beings. Jehovah/Allah is not only the chief tempter of gullible humans on earth, he is also highly irritable, unforgiving, lawless, and blundering. He tempted Job through the fictitious devil, which was but an innate part of himself. According to him, he was only tempting Abraham when he incited him to slaughter and burn his own innocent child. And he tempted Jesus Christ by trying to lure him into joining his council of wicked earthbound principalities to derail his redemptive mission in the world.

And when Jehovah/Allah willfully tormented and massacred the entire helpless population of the Jewish Exodus in the wilderness, his argument was that they repeatedly offended him. Thus, he argued that he was justified to retaliate against them with evil. A God that has reasons to do evil is simply not in tune with the divine norm of perfection. What we hear throughout the ill-fated Jewish desert trek is "**and the anger of Jehovah was kindled,**" as he routinely harassed and massacred the defenseless people.

In fact, Jehovah/Allah is a premediated evil spirit. 'Unconditional love for all' is certainly not in his nature. The distance between Goshen in Egypt and the so-called Promised Land in Canaan was less than 200 miles but Jehovah/Allah purposely caused the helpless Jewish Exodus to wander about in the hash wilderness hungry, thirsty, and sick for a whole 40 years till they all perished.

Moses later explained to the battered *new* generation that survived the ill-fated Exodus that "Jehovah your God has led you these forty years in the wilderness, **that he might humble you**, testing you to know what was in your heart, whether you would keep his commandments, or not. **And he humbled you and let you hunger.**" [Deuteronomy 8:2-3]

The Scripture captures the heavy-handed response of Jehovah on one occasion when the starving, battered population ventured to express their privation and anguish. The book of Numbers narrates: "And the people complained in the hearing of Jehovah about their misfortunes; and when Jehovah heard it, **his anger was kindled**, and the [ravaging] fire of Jehovah burned among them, and consumed some outlying parts of the camp." And though Jehovah eventually sent an excess number of quails (migratory game birds) to them for meat, the narrative says that "while the meat was yet between their teeth, before it was consumed, **the**

anger of Jehovah was kindled against the people, and Jehovah smote the people with a very great plague." [Numbers 11:1, 33]

Finally, at the end of the gruesome desert trek, Jehovah had premeditatedly horrified and massacred the entire defenseless population of Israelites who trusted that he was leading them out of Egypt to a certain Promised Land. Numbers 26:64-65 reads, "But among these there was not a man [saved] of those numbered by Moses and Aaron the priest, who had numbered the people of Israel in the wilderness of Sinai [at the start of the ill-fated Exodus]. For Jehovah had said of them, 'They shall [all] die in the wilderness.' There was not left a man of them, except Caleb the son of Jephunneh and Joshua the son of Nun."

Of course, Jehovah/Allah never minced words in saying that he is wrathful and unreliable. He is a tempter, a jealous, and an unforgiving God who can never resist visiting evil on those who, as little as, show displeasure with his ungodly ways. He said clearly to his Jewish victims, "I Jehovah your God am a jealous God, visiting the iniquity of the fathers upon the children to the third and the fourth generation of those who hate me." Thus, Moses warned the people about finding any fault with Jehovah's evil ways. "For Jehovah your God in the midst of you is a jealous God," said Moses to the lost sons of Adam, "lest the anger of Jehovah your God be kindled against you, and he destroy you from off the face of the earth. [Exodus 20:5; Deuteronomy 6:15]

It is clear from the Scripture that the spirit is divinely indissoluble. Therefore, the death of any spirit is not like the death of the mortal man. When a man dies, his mortal body decomposes completely and returns to the various elements of organic matter from where it evolved. The dead body thus totally dissolves back into its original mineral constituents, and nothing of those dissolved constituents can ever resemble the person.

The death of a spirit, on the contrary, refers to loss of spiritual potentials due to automatic detachment from his divine Source rather than outright dissolution. When the sinful spirit dies, he is not automatically "dissolved" or re-assimilated into the perfect Father from whom he emanated. Rather, he is automatically spewed out of the perfect heavenly household. He literally falls far away from his Perfect Origin because he has become polluted and incompatible. He sinks into the Outer Darkness and ceases to epitomize true light, life, love and holiness.

Thus, a dead spirit continues to "live" in the Outer Darkness, howbeit as a Fatherless spirit, and as a shadow of his true self. The Scripture tells the story better in the book of Jude where it reports that "the angels that did not keep their original position [in the Father's heavenly household] but forsook their own proper dwelling place he has reserved with eternal bonds under dense darkness for the judgment of the great day." [Jude 6 (NWT)] The Scripture adds that all spirits in the world sinned and "fall short of the Father's eternal glory." It says, "everyone has sinned; we all fall short of the Father's glorious standard." [Romans 3:23(NLT)]

A fallen dead spirit can be likened to a dead car battery that can no longer fulfill its real purpose, even though it continues to give out a very dim glow on the car dashboard. Better still, the fallen dead spirit is more like a defective electrical appliance. He does not only lack the ability to exhibit his full and proper potential, but he has also become destructive in all his intents and purposes.

Thus, a fallen dead spirit must be recharged or rekindled and made to conform to the Father's perfect heavenly standards before he can be readmitted into the heavenly household, or he will remain dead forever in the Outer Darkness. Only Jesus Christ can and has the Father's mandate to rekindle any repentant spirits in the world because he is a truly living spirit. And he says, "You, therefore, must be perfect, as your heavenly Father is perfect." [Matthew 5:48]

The group of spirits that groped their way in the watery dark abyss "in the beginning" of our makeshift universal mushroom were the dislocated spirits alluded to in the book of Jude. They were the band of overambitious spirits who thought that perfection was a hindrance to "real enjoyment" and that eternal life and happiness can possibly exist outside the Father and beyond the *proper* dwelling place of perfect spirits.

As the diagram on page 11 clearly shows, the big bright sphere represents a harmonious whole. The Father's perfect spiritual Kingdom remains one and intact. The Father continues to be the only one true King both in the glorious heavenly Kingdom and in entire existence. Every being within the heavenly Kingdom remains a living son or prince to the sole eternal King, while the overambitious sons and princes that willfully forsook the heavenly household remain eternally dead and lost in the overwhelming Outer Darkness.

The dead spirits had immediate and perpetual needs within the Outer Darkness, which are directly related to the divine potentials that they once had but lost as fallen sons of light. First, they needed alternative kinds of light, to illuminate both their ambience and their inner selves. Without light, they could not even begin to rationalize their exact situation to adapt to their eternal predicaments. They needed to generate another *home* for themselves because they had literally become "homeless" spirits. And they must evolve another kind of life with its forms of artificial intelligence, creativity, and pleasures suitable for their "new" habitation. All these would represent false versions of the divine attributes that they had taken for granted while in the heavenly household. More especially, they must evolve conducive biospheres with appropriate ecosystems within which to exert their newfound *projected* personalities.

All the fallen, dead spirits that found themselves within the spiritual "nether gloom," as reported in Jude 6, felt the same handicaps, and shared the same natural needs. The fallen spirits of Jehovah/Allah, the so-called archangels and gods of the world, the captive *jinn* and humans as well as all other mortal beings in the universe; all bore the full consequences of spiritual death "in the beginning." Jehovah/Allah's fallen dead spirit was not on a different plane within the nether region, nor was he of a different form from the rest of us. "There is no distinction [whatsoever]; since all have sinned and fall short of the glory of the Father," says Romans 3:23.

Karen Armstrong wrote:

> "The first man [Adam] had been created from the substance of a god [i.e. of a pre-existent spirit or animating life force]: he therefore shared the divine nature, in however limited a way. There was no gulf between human beings and the gods [Jehovah/Allah and the so-called archangels]. The natural world, men and women and the gods themselves all shared the same nature and derived from the same divine substance. ... The gods were not shut off from the human race in a separate, ontological sphere: divinity was not essentially different from humanity. ... The gods and human beings shared the same predicaments, the only difference being that the gods were more powerful. ..." [Karen Armstrong; *A History of God*, pg. 9]

The spirits of the gods were not necessarily more powerful than the human spirits. They rather outwitted and usurped the powers of the less informed humans, in the same way that devious individuals outwit and enslave the less fortunate and guileless ones in human societies today. By successfully denying ignorant humans the basic knowledge of good and evil, the so-called gods tactically desensitized and enslaved them for life. And only direct intervention from the Father's mercy seat can free humankind from eternal captivity in their hand.

As we already know, imperfection, opportunism and foul play are hallmarks of the world of corrupt spirits in the Outer Darkness. The most powerful are not necessarily the most sensible or knowledgeable in the world. The President of America, for instance, may hardly be the most intelligent and honorable man in the USA, yet he rules over multitudes of renowned intellectuals, wise, and reputable men and women. Such a man would simply be a political opportunist who merely outmaneuvered other men and women of like ambitions that coveted the same position of political authority.

Jehovah/Allah is in no real way more intelligent or powerful than any other spirit on planet Earth. He is perhaps the most ruthless opportunist. In fact, his actions and utterances show clearly that he is the most perverse and obstinate spirit on planet Earth. If he were reasonable, he would have realized the futility of his dominion ambitions in the Outer Darkness, of throwing away his perfect spiritual heritage in the Father for a bungling life of falsehood in the region of spiritual darkness, chaos and lifelessness.

All the fallen dead spirits in the netherworlds are prodigal sons of the Father. Like the proverbial prodigal son, they all have *only* two options, which is made possible by the Father's steadfast love and grace. The Father has granted them the opportunity of outright spiritual rebirth. So, they can individually appraise their "new" situation and overall state in the netherworlds and willingly choose to repent and return to the Father who has never stopped loving them. They can individually choose to regain true eternal life and their pride of place in the Father's heavenly household. Or they can knowingly choose to remain dead and languish in the Outer Darkness forever.

Sadly, Jehovah/Allah did not only choose the second option, but he also chose to oppose the Father's will in the world by working so hard to prevent humans from freely exercising their individual rights to choose the right option. Thus, even in death, Jehovah/Allah still harbors the ulterior intentions of eventually outmaneuvering and enslaving the rest of the fallen spirits on planet Earth, to enthrone himself as *God Almighty* over his less-informed brethren. But even though Jehovah/Allah poses as *God Almighty* and sole creator of the entire universe to ignorant humans, he is just an unrepentant wayward spirit. And talking about the creation of the universe, we all contributed directly, and still contribute toward the endless remaking of our common primordial situation.

The make-believe Genesis story of creation in the Jewish Torah represents Jehovah/Allah's simplistic attempt at permanently obscuring empirical facts about the observable universe. Firstly, he implied that he single-handedly created the entire universe. Then, he sold the erroneous impression that he created the human spirit by breathing into the nostrils of a sculpted clay image of man. But he is a fallen dead spirit and cannot give life. Such a task is even far beyond the scope of truly living spirits in heaven. All spirits emanated from the Father and only he has the power to create, reabsorb or eternally cast out a fallen dead spirit into the Outer Darkness. Hence, Jesus Christ spoke of the Father as **the only one "who can** destroy both spirit and body in hell." [Matthew 10:28]

The Quran tries to lend credence to Jehovah/Allah's lies by saying that even Jesus Christ sculpted a bird from mud and breathed into it *by Allah's permission* and it flew away. Quran 5:110 reads, "Allah saith: O Jesus, son of Mary! Remember My favour unto thee and unto thy mother; how I strengthened thee with the holy Spirit, so that thou spakest unto mankind in the cradle as in maturity; and how I taught thee the Scripture and Wisdom and the Torah and the Gospel; **and how thou didst shape of clay as it were the likeness of a bird by *My permission*, and didst blow upon it and it was a bird by *My permission*,** and thou didst heal him who was born blind and the leper by *My permission*; and how thou didst raise the dead, by *My permission* and how I restrained the Children of Israel from (harming) thee when thou camest unto them with clear proofs, and those of them who disbelieved exclaimed: This is naught else than mere magic."

To believe that Jehovah created Adam by blowing his corrupted breath into the nostrils of a clay sculpture is both blind and lame. As I normally say to people, it was rather Abraham that created Jehovah/Allah by dusting up a homeless desert hermit, endorsing, and emboldening him to start claiming to be God. The three-sister Abrahamic religious cults—Judaism, customary Christianity and Islam—ultimately perfected Jehovah/Allah's metamorphoses and character laundering. They are the ones who brought him to limelight and made him not only the sole *creator* of the universe, but also a transcendent *God Almighty*.

Thus, Jehovah/Allah is absolutely nobody without human beings. He is entirely inconsequential without the throng of *blind and lame* religious bigots that suppress the masses, common sense, and voices of reason in attempt to give meaning to his wayward ambitions. The same is true of tyrants and brutal rulers of nations who serve Jehovah/Allah's ulterior interests on earth. They too derive their undue powers from ruthless armed armies that are trained to sheepishly suppress the voices of reason and shield them from righteous uprising by the masses. Furthermore, it is still human beings that created or built New York City, for instance, not Jehovah/Allah, the false king of the world. He is but a colonial master.

All spirits in the universe, including captive human spirits, are eternal because they emanated from the Father who is eternal Divine Spirit. They all existed as individual spirits in the Father's heavenly household before the fall and in the primordial prison of total darkness before the big bang that created the universe. They all continue to exist as individual spirits in the world and must work out their personal salvations as individuals.

According to the Quran, "Each spirit earneth only on its own account, nor doth any laden bear another's load." ... "Whosoever goeth right, it is only for (the good of) his own spirit that he goeth right, and whosoever erreth, erreth only to its hurt. No laden spirit can bear another's load." [Quran 6:164; 17:15] The Bible also affirms that "The spirit that sins shall die. The son shall not suffer for the iniquity of the father, nor the father suffer for the iniquity of the son; the righteousness of the righteous shall be upon himself, and the wickedness of the wicked shall be upon himself." [Ezekiel 18:20]

The Genesis creation fable that deliberately speaks of Jehovah and the so-called archangels as if they were the only spirits that were caught up in the primordial dark abyss before the said creation is a very malicious lie. Human spirits were there too, as were innumerable other fallen spirits that today jointly animate the universe. Creation of the universe was a collective achievement of the entire heavenly dropouts. Keeping it going is still the collective responsibility of all and sundry. In fact, without amalgamating their remnant energies 'in the beginning,' the fallen dead spirits could not have been able to trigger the cataclysmic explosion that gave them temporary respite from the pitch-darkness of their primordial arena. They still cannot do without one another, even to this day.

So, every spirit in existence, whether living or dead, is ageless because all spirits emanated from the Father who is eternal Divine Spirit. As we already know, spirits that sin die spiritually; they do not become younger or non-existent at death. This means that all the fallen dead spirits in the world, including captive human spirits, existed before the foundation of Jehovah/Allah's fictitious creation. Most certainly, the corrupt, dead breath of Jehovah/Allah can neither create true life nor rekindle a dead spirit within the lifeless realm of darkness.

All organic lifeforms are generated out of cosmic dust as encoded in the primordial blueprint. They are projected animations of fallen dead spirits. They serve to help them mimic divine activities to have a false sense of *living* in their present region of death. This applies equally to Jehovah/Allah and his ignorant religious devotees. In fact, the Bible says that Jehovah/Allah and his human slaves share exact "image and likeness," meaning they share exact nature and conditions within their shared universal prison of darkness.

The earlier that human beings understand that Jehovah/Allah, the bungling god of Eden, is a big fraud the better would be our prospect of realizing the whole truth. The better would be our chances of making the right choice between spiritual resurrection by Jesus Christ and languishing in eternal self-damnation in the Outer Darkness.

Jehovah/Allah is not *God Almighty* but a powerless impostor. He is neither our perfect loving Father in heaven nor Jesus Christ our Redeemer. He certainly does not share the same perfect qualities with the Father and his Son Jesus Christ. The Scripture counsels that we should knowingly resist and overcome him to find eternal life. James 4:7 says, "Submit yourselves therefore to the Father. Resist [Jehovah/Allah] the devil and he will flee from you."

Certainly, humans did not voluntarily allow Jehovah/Allah to build his false and selfish kingdom over their dislocated spirits. "In the beginning," the consensus was for a collective effort toward generating a *new home* out of our common debilitating situation where all the fallen spirits would at least, be "free and happy," not where the few would forcibly enslave the many. Unfortunately, that was precisely what the world without the Father turned out to be.

Wicked spirits that were shrewder and more violent in thought and action soon dominated the stage, and the winners took it all. Jehovah/Allah, being a very cunning and ruthless opportunist, stealthily dominated the stage on planet Earth. He first employed deceit and falsehood and gained peoples' undivided allegiance. Then, he enthroned himself as *God Almighty* through divide-and-rule tactics, outright lawlessness, and violence in actions and utterances. "For had it not been for Allah's [tactic of] repelling some men by means of others," says Quran 22:40 "cloisters and churches and oratories and mosques, wherein the name of Allah is oft mentioned, would assuredly have been pulled down."

Much like all human tyrants, Jehovah/Allah ultimately turned uninformed, trusting humans into captives and religious slaves. He now has humans in eternal religious straitjackets that no captive human spirit can ever undo without the superior help of the Divine Messiah. Jehovah/Allah attempted to use Adam and Eve as guinea pigs to perfect the straightjackets of ignorance and he almost succeeded. But the right and timely help from our loving heavenly Father reached them in the person of the redeeming heavenly Christ who appeared to them as Divine Spirit of Knowledge. He rekindled their blindfolded spirits and set them free from the straightjackets of ignorance that Jehovah/Allah had craftily imposed on their spirits. Jesus Christ works still to do the same for Adam's posterity and indeed all captive spirits in the world.

Humans have always been the worst for trusting Jehovah/Allah, who the Scripture cryptically refers to as a "a Great Red Dragon, with seven heads," "the Beast that was and is not," and "that Ancient Serpent, who is called the Devil and Satan, the Deceiver of the whole world." [Revelation 12:3, 9; 17:11] The battle for the spiritual salvation of our captive spirits has raged on since the victory of Adam and Eve in Eden, between Jehovah/Allah the Devil and Jesus Christ our heavenly Redeemer whom the Scripture also cryptically refers to as "the Lamb."

Revelation 17:13-14 reports that the seven crowned heads of the great red dragon gave over their powers to *the beast that was a living spirit but now dead* for the purpose of fighting against the heavenly Christ as a united force. It reads, "These are of one mind and give over their power and authority to the beast;" so that "they will make war on the Lamb, and the Lamb will conquer them, ... and those with him [true Christ followers] are called and chosen and faithful."

Remarkably, the Devil tempted Jesus Christ to accept rulership role in the world, thus confirming that Jehovah/Allah is really the Devil and that the seven crowned dragons indeed gave over their powers to him as the consolidated ruler of their joint earthly kingdoms. Luke 4:5-6 reads, "And the Devil took him [Jesus Christ] up and showed him all the kingdoms of the world in a moment of time, and said to him, 'To you I will give all this authority and their glory; **for it has been delivered to me**, and I give it to whom I will."

I am sure that any human being who understands these facts clearly will strive to become like Adam and Eve. Indeed, the type of courage and bravery that Adam and Eve exhibited in that ancient garden of ignorance could have only come by the special grace of the Father, and by the superior power of knowledge that the heavenly Christ imparted into their spirits. Jesus Christ makes it certain that his true followers still need the same courage of rock, even in our present age. Jehovah/Allah is a deadly adversary. So, spiritual salvation is indeed a tough battle.

Indeed, any situation that promotes one person as the *ruler* and the rest as the *subjects* is evil. Such a situation existed in Eden. And such a situation will unavoidably be oppressive. Accordingly, Jehovah/Allah declares himself *God*, *King* and *Lord* over humankind, while "sitting in the heavens and resting his feet on the heads of human beings on the earth." Quran 11:7 says that Jehovah/Allah "created the heavens and the earth in six days," and then established his throne of oppression "upon the waters." And Revelation 17:15 explains that "the waters" upon which Jehovah/Allah's throne rests "are [captive spirits of] peoples and multitudes and nations and tongues." Isaiah 40:22(NLT) on its part, records that Jehovah/Allah "sits above the circle of the earth. The people below seem like grasshoppers to him!" So, the scriptures are unanimous that Jehovah/Allah is a usurper, an oppressor and a lawless entity. His human ruling agents on earth follow his precise examples.

But Jesus Christ assures his true followers of ultimate victory in the end. However, he also wants them to be adequately prepared to play their own parts. "Whoever does not bear his own cross and come after me, cannot be my disciple," he says to them. ... "For whoever would [seek to] save his life [of this world] will lose it; and whoever loses his life for my sake, he will save [exchange] it [for eternal life]." ... "Or what king, going to encounter another king in war, will not sit down first and take counsel whether he is able with ten thousand to meet him who comes against him with twenty thousand? And if not, while the other is yet a great way off, he sends an embassy and asks terms of peace." [Luke 14:27; 9:24; 14:31-32]

Finally, Jehovah/Allah and his accomplices have not had it easy since Eden, for as he says himself, "There is no peace for the wicked." [Isaiah 48:22] Every tyrant always suffers his own Waterloo at the height of his celebrated atrocities, and Jehovah/Allah will not be an exception. Jesus Christ is working still against his oppressive world order to set free all willing captives spirits in the world. He tells his true followers that the battle will be tough and painful, "But not a hair of your head will perish. By your endurance you will gain your lives." ... "In the world you have tribulation; but be of good cheer, **I have overcome the world**." [Luke 21:18-19; John 16:33]

THE SO-CALLED KINGDOMS OF THE WORLD

Ezekiel 18:20 has revealed to us the 'principle of perfection,' as it pertains to the perfect heavenly Kingdom of the Father and to the perfect spirits that dwell therein. It reads, "The spirit that sins shall die!" We have also seen from the Scripture that the death of a spirit is not like the death of the mortal human body. The spirit that dies instantly forfeits his place in the realm of perfection and falls into the overwhelming Outer Darkness. He continues to exist or *live*, within the region of spiritual death, completely stripped of all his perfect attributes. The divine norm of perfection does not apply to the world because it is not a part of the Father's realm of perfection.

The Scripture has also revealed to us in Jude 6 the practical position and dilemma of the overambitious spirits that violated the heavenly norm of perfection and died. It reads, "And the angels who did not keep their original position but forsook their own proper dwelling place he has **reserved with eternal bonds under dense darkness** for the judgment of the great day." [Jude 6 (NWT)]

The two simple scriptural verses above tell us almost everything we ought to know about the rebellious, fallen spirits. **"They did not keep their original position,"** means that they willfully broke their original commitment to the heavenly norm of perfection. They knew the consequences or wages of such reckless action. Every living spirit in the realm of perfection knows that. So, the said fallen angels knowingly **"forsook their own proper dwelling place"** and were instantaneously spewed out of the Father's divine presence. They could not possibly continue to dwell in the realm of perfection when they had willfully rejected the perfect heavenly standards.

Being **"reversed with eternal bonds [or chains] under dense darkness"** means utter limitations. They were restricted in their corrupted potentials as dead spirits and by the overpowering darkness of their alien environment. However, being **reserved "for the judgment of the great [last] day"** shows that the Father had not quite given up on all of them. Although they ought to have died eternally and forgotten, the Father granted a "second chance" to any of them that would show genuine repentance.

The Father did not sentence them to outright eternal self-condemnation but **reserved** them in an interim atmosphere of grace to try to retrieve as many as would see reason and wish to return to their pride of place in the Kingdom. In this, we can readily glimpse the infinite love of the Father and his divine will for the ultimate resurrection of all his fallen sons in the world. "It is not my heavenly Father's will that even one of these little ones should perish," says Jesus Christ our Redeemer. [Matthew 18:14(NLT)]

Naturally, the spirits that sinned died forever, but the infinite nature of the Father's love obliged him to initiate measures for the ultimate redemption and resurrection of repentant ones. Hence, the Father commissioned the divine mission of Jesus Christ for the world. John 3:16-18 says, "For the Father so loved [his fallen sons in] the world that he gave [sent] his only Son, that whoever believes in him [in his offer of divine amnesty] should not perish but have [regain] eternal life. For the Father sent the Son into the world, not to condemn the world, but that the world might be saved through him. He who believes in him is not condemned; he who does not believe is [self-]condemned already."

The book of Romans further says, "This was to show the Father's righteousness, because in his divine forbearance he had passed over former sins; it was to prove at the present time that he himself is righteous and that he justifies him who has faith in Jesus [Christ]. ... [So,] While we were still weak, at the right time Christ died for the ungodly. ... But God shows his love for us in that while we were yet sinners Christ died for us." [Romans 3:25-26; 5:6, 8]

Finally, earlier disciples of Jesus Christ who fully understood the Father's grace and plan of salvation through Jesus Christ also testified. "And this is the testimony," says 1 John 5:11-12, "that the Father gave us eternal life, and this life is in his Son. He who has the Son has life; he who has not the Son of the Father has not life." It is as simple as that!

Jesus Christ used the parables of '*the Lost Sheep*," "*the Lost Coin*" and "*the Lost Son*" to explain to us the real situation confronting all fallen dead spirits in the world and to help us understand the special love and divine will of the Father for all of them. Sadly, human beings read the parables as irrelevant homilies. They find it hard to understand that they are indeed the *lost* sons of the Father that Jesus Christ seeks to retrieve from the world of darkness. Most human beings already know that their real selves are the unseen spirits that animate their mortal clay bodies. But they still find it so hard to appreciate that their spirits are indeed corrupted and lost both in their mortal earthen bodies and within the dark universe.

Our expanding universe erupted out of total darkness within the infinite realm of Darkness. It persists in total darkness because it is devoid of Divine Light. The Scripture confirms that by saying that "The world is a dark place, and its people [all the heavenly dropouts in it] have no light." [2 Esdras 14:20 (GNB)] But although human beings know these facts, they still find it hard to see themselves as "the people" that dwell in "the dark world." They still find it hard to understand that they are really the fallen spirits that the Father had *reserved* in the deep dark region for ultimate reform.

Again, 1 John 1:5(NLT) says that "the Father is Light, and there is no darkness in him at all." And 1 Timothy 6:16 describes the Father as the Sovereign King "who alone has immortality and dwells in unapproachable Light, whom no man has ever seen or can see." Yet human beings have also refused to appreciate the fact that our loving heavenly Father, who is eternal, infinite Divine Light, cannot possibly be the groping inventor of our world of darkness. He cannot also be the sneaky Jehovah/Allah who dwells happily in insurmountable darkness in the world, who says that he would in fact, "continue to dwell in thick darkness" to all eternity.

Anyway, from Ezekiel 18:20, Jude 6, and 2 Peter 2:4, let us move straight to the very genesis of our present world of darkness. The very first two verses of the Hebrew Torah tell us the story of how the fallen spirits tried to improvise their nether region. "In the beginning," the group of dislocated spirits groped their way in the watery, dark abyss. They were visibly incapacitated, confused, and hopeless. Like wayward crew members, they willfully stepped off the secure deck of the Father's heavenly Ship of State and instantaneously sank to the bottomless watery deep in the Outer Darkness.

But while the wayward heavenly crew forsook their secure state and were instantly swallowed up by eternal darkness, the

Father's heavenly Ship of State remained infinite, harmonious and on course. The rebellious spirits sinned and died. Their action and its recompense did not rub off on the upright spirits onboard, neither did they tarnish or cause the heavenly Ship of State to alter course. For, as the Quran says, "Whosoever goeth right, it is only for (the good of) his own spirit that he goeth right, and whosoever erreth, erreth only to its hurt. No laden spirit can bear another's load." [Quran 17:15]

So, the heavenly Kingdom of the Father remained a perfect heaven for the worthy spirits that continued to conform to its norm of perfection. The Father remained eternal King in his glorious Kingdom and his perfect princes continued to bask in his eternal glory.

The Scripture says that "the wages of sin is death." So, the first two verses of the Bible capture the instant wages of the original sins of the heavenly dropouts. They suddenly plunged into eternal darkness, and became Fatherless, homeless, and utterly incapacitated. To their utter disappointment, they suddenly learnt in a very bitter way that eternal order, blissful existence, and peace of mind could not exist without the Father. They also suddenly realized that they were totally on their own and had to try to address some of their immediate handicaps.

Firstly, they badly needed ambient light of any sort. Then, they needed another home or a conducive atmosphere within which to try to invent a kind of life that could serve as an alternative to outright spiritual death. The physical outcome of their collective exertion within the primordial darkness was this chaotic material universe, which will ultimately die and revert to total darkness as it was "in the beginning." They also invented an illusory type of life that is both distracting and detrimental to their ultimate spiritual reform.

Even though the Father made adequate contingency provisions for his fallen sons to facilitate their spiritual reform within their interim quarantine, they opted for the wrong trajectory because of their rebellious mindset. The Father purposely allowed them remnant light energy that collectively harnessed, was sufficient for righteous aspirations. But everything they invented turned out to be evil because of greed and selfish ambitions.

The craftier ones schemed to have the upper hand over others, and they became self-seeking leaders and ultimately dominated and enslaved the less privileged. Darkness persisted in their overall situation. Vices proliferated and became the lifestyle of their false existence. Hence, their overall inventions became mere illusions that distracted rather than exhorted them to expected virtuous ambitions and spiritual regeneration.

Thus, even Jehovah/Allah confesses that the life of the world is but comfort of illusion. "Beautified for mankind is the love of the joys (that come) from women and offspring, and store-up heaps of gold and silver, and horses branded (with their mark), and cattle and land," he says. "This is comfort of the life of the world. ... **"The life of this world is but comfort of illusion**." [Quran 2:14, 185]

As the diagram shows, the little dark circle *below* the Father's glorious Kingdom represents the imperfect, finite material universe that the fallen dead spirits orchestrated within the infinite Outer Darkness. The whole universe is really a very tiny dark hut within the infinite realm of total darkness. Human beings see the universe as wonderful and everlasting and call it a creation of our perfect heavenly Father because they lack knowledge. But since the heavenly Christ imported the forbidden knowledge of good and evil into Eden, people are increasingly discerning the truth.

The Scripture announced that "The true light that enlightens every man was coming into the world." [John 1:9] And at the appointed time, Jesus Christ appeared amongst us and affirmed his presence. "I am the light of the world," he said; "he who follows me will not walk in darkness but will have the light of life." [John 8:12] He came as true light into the universe to help blindfolded spirits appreciate the eternal difference that exists between divine light and the false lights of our dark universe.

And "The light shines in the darkness, and the darkness has not [can never] overcome it," says John 1:5. In fact, our inspired scientists bear witness to the true light, as they progressively resolve the mysteries of the creation of our expanding universe. They are providing modern humans with empirical evidence that are increasingly helping enlightened minds to fully understand Christ's gospel of the difference.

Any human being that acquires adequate divine knowledge should be able to interpret Genesis 1:1-2 in its true light:

> "In the beginning, when *Elohim* [the fallen dead spirits] created the universe, the earth was formless and desolate. The raging ocean that covered everything was engulfed in **total darkness**, and the power of *Elohim* [the fallen dead spirits] was moving over the water." [Genesis 1:1-2(TEV)]

The following are immediately discernable from the two straightforward verses:

- The creation in question was the expanding universe within which we now live and die as human beings. The so-called "heavens and earth" merely refer to stars, planets and other celestial bodies existing within the universal mushroom. They are not in any way referring to the Father's true spiritual Heaven, which we now know exists beyond this material realm of darkness.

- The said creation took place within a deep, dark watery arena, which incidentally perfectly describes the primordial state of the "Outer Darkness" within which the Father had *reserved* the fallen dead spirits.

- The entire group of groping *Elohim* or so-called *Gods* involved with the said creation were completely trapped and incapacitated within the overwhelming darkness. Neither the Father nor the heavenly Christ was ever trapped in darkness because they are *eternal* Light. In fact, they dwell eternally in "unapproachable light."

- As expected, the planet Earth that was conjured out of the overwhelming thick darkness was both "without form" and spiritually "void."

- It should be noted that the primordial deep, dark watery *reserve* had both form and divine purpose though. It was the cataclysmic eruption that the groping spirits triggered out of the primordial arena that was "without form" and spiritually "void" as it was characterized by chaos and imbalance of forces. The imperfect nature of the said creation offers clear proof that the groping spirits no longer possessed perfect divine abilities.

A legend has it that the groping spirits hovered hopelessly in primordial darkness for a whole *ten mystical days* before the fictitious *six days* of creation. That meant that the dark watery *reserve* indeed offered the fallen dead spirits ample time and adequate opportunities for serious reflection, repentance, and corrective actions. But they chose to focus their remnant energies on their original rebellious intents of creating a world of sensual pleasure.

The Scripture did not leave humans in doubt about the true nature of the groping spirits in the Genesis creation story. There is no scriptural basis whatsoever for anyone to believe that Jehovah/Allah was the sole creator of the universe. Neither does the Genesis creation account say or even imply that the spirit of Jehovah/Allah was dwelling in "unapproachable light" before the "let there be light" outburst by the groping spirits.

The Scripture rather shows clearly that Jehovah/Allah was one of the groping spirits stranded in total darkness "in the beginning" and in fact, stresses that he continues to dwell permanently in thick darkness even to this day. "Jehovah has set the sun in the heavens but has said that he would [continue to] dwell in thick darkness," says 1 King 8:12. Psalms 18:11 rephrases the same fact by saying that "He [Jehovah/Allah] made darkness his covering around him, his canopy thick clouds dark with water."

What people should be wondering about is why Jehovah/Allah or any right-thinking entity would frantically invoke light out his prison of darkness and still prefer to continue dwelling in thick darkness, especially when Genesis 1:4 says that he himself saw and confirmed "that the light was good." Could Jehovah/Allah really afford to dwell in the light but knowingly refuse to do so?

Well, Jesus Christ supplies the right answer to that. Jehovah/Allah prefers to dwell in thick darkness because his deeds are evil. "For everyone who does evil hates the light, and does not come to the light, lest his deeds should be exposed," he says. "But he who does what is true comes to the light, that it may be clearly seen that his deeds have been wrought in the Father [who is Divine Light]." [John 3:20-21]

Furthermore, the Genesis creation account clearly depicts the said creation as a joint venture by a group of groping spirits, which it collectively refers to as *Elohim*. But Jehovah/Allah now claims to be the sole inventor of the universe, and religious believers see nothing dubious about that. Even then, the Genesis account portrays the groping spirits as collaborating equals that deliberated and agreed on every aspect of whatever they did.

In fact, the inventors acted strictly as a gang of equals. It was always, "**Let us** make man in our image, after our likeness; ...

"Behold, the man has become like one of us, ... "Come, **let us** go down, and there confuse their [humans] language, that they may not understand one another's speech."[Genesis 1:26; 3:22; 11:7]

On a more realistic stage, the Scripture captures Jehovah/Allah as a mere homeless desert hermit that wandered about the mountainous Middle Eastern "howling waste of the wilderness" on planet Earth. Indeed, Abram first encountered Jehovah/Allah face to face as a homeless, easygoing magic-working mountain hermit by the Oaks of Mamre on a high hill in Shechem and called him El-Shaddai, meaning a 'mountain god.' Certainly, neither Adam, nor Abram encountered a true *God Almighty* that dwells "in unapproachable light."

Again, Jehovah/Allah claims to be the sole God of the earthly world, but the Scripture faults that claim outright. The Scripture makes it clear that Jehovah/Allah is just one among seven other wicked, self-seeking earthbound principalities that literally colonized and rule over ignorant humans on planet Earth. So, Jehovah/Allah is merely the ceremonial head of the council of wicked principalities whose jurisdictions are strictly restricted to the earthly world of humans.

Deuteronomy 32:8-9 is very clear on the fact that Jehovah/Allah is but a tutelary deity among other tutelary deities that arrogated to themselves authority over allotted territories and tribes of peoples on planet Earth. It reads, "When the Most High [ceremonial head of the gods of the world] apportioned the nations, when he divided mankind, he fixed the boundaries of the peoples according to the number of the [collaborating] gods; **Jehovah's own portion** was his people, Jacob **his allotted share**." [Deuteronomy 32:8-9 (NRSV)]

The New Revised Standard Version (NRSV) footnotes on above verses are equally explicit. The so-called Most High stands for the "traditional rendering of Hebrew *Elyon.*" But that was merely a crafty derivative of another Hebrew word *Elohim*, which is the plural form of *El*, meaning *god*. There is no reasonable basis therefore, for people to assume that *Elohim*, as used in the Genesis creation fable, implies that Jehovah/Allah is not an individual spirit but multiple entities in one body. *Elohim* rightly refers to the "Let Us" group of individual groping spirits or *gods* that stand out clearly in the narrative.

In the beginning, none of the fallen spirits was confused about the fact that they were all individual spirits, princes, gods, or angelic sons of the Father. Jehovah/Allah and the so-called archangels merely attached false prefixes to their natural status to make them appear topmost and superior to the rest of their fallen brethren on planet Earth. Propelled by greed and hierarchy spirit, they instinctively made themselves "most high gods," "chief princes," "arch angels," "highest chiefs," and so on, just to feel a false air of importance over the rest of us.

At first, the greedy haughty ones did not deem it necessary to dispute or distort the fact that the rest of us remained gods, princes and angels. Obviously, where there are "most high gods," "chief princes," and "arch angels," there must also be "ordinary" gods, princes and angels. But with the successful eradication of the humans' divine right to knowledge that was perfected in the Garden of Eden, the so-called *most high* gods tactically denied the fallen human spirits even their natural status as "ordinary" gods, princes and angels. The Genesis creation fable blatantly denies the preexistence of human spirits. It simply says that humans beings are inconsequential clay sculptures that are powered by the corrupted breath of Jehovah/Allah. That is utterly evil!

Sadly, that malicious lie has since *stuck like Chuck* in the psyche of ignorant human beings. Even when Jehovah/Allah later confessed that we are, indeed, all gods, he still maintained that he would make us all die believing that we are just mortal human beings. His words in Psalms 82:6-7 reads, "I say, 'You are [indeed] gods, sons of the Most High [the Father], **all of you**; nevertheless, you shall die like men [who do not know that they are gods and princes] and fall like any prince."

The actual wording of the Hebrew Genesis reads, **"In the beginning *Elohim* created the heavens and the earth."** The text did not use *El* or *God* but *Elohim*, which is the plural of the word *El*, because it was speaking about a group of *Els*. Surely, writers of the Hebrew texts knew the difference between *Elohim* and *El*. Doctored English versions of the Bible later changed the word Elohim to God, thereby giving the word a singular meaning to support the blatant lie that Jehovah/Allah was the sole creator of the universe.

It was such criminal alterations that ultimately emboldened and gave Jehovah/Allah the impetus to openly start claiming to be the only God in existence. "I am Jehovah, who made all things," he says. "**I alone** stretched out the heavens. Who was with me when I made the earth?" ... "I am the First and the Last; **there is no other God.**" [Isaiah 44:24, 6(NLT)]

Evidently, Jehovah expects ignorant humans to accept that he was just a mysterious lone ranger, telling himself "Let Us" do this and that during his fictitious six-day creation. But he briefly forgets his own storyline in Deuteronomy 32:8-9 where he refers to himself as the *Most High* among the gods. So, Psalms 82:1(TEV) maintains that "Jehovah presides in the heavenly council; **in the assembly of the gods**, he gives his decision." And Moses asks in Exodus 15:11, "Who is like thee, O Jehovah, **among the gods**?"

Furthermore, **Karen Armstrong** wrote:

> "When they recite the *Shema* today, Jews give it a monotheistic interpretation: Jehovah our God is One and unique. [But] The Deuteronomist had not yet reached this perspective [when the actual Hebrew Genesis account was written]. 'Jehovah *ehad*' did not mean [*Elohim*] is One, but that Jehovah was the only deity whom it was permitted [for the Jews] to worship. Other gods were still a threat: their cults were attractive and could lure Israelites from Jehovah, who was a jealous God. If they obeyed Jehovah's laws, he

would bless them and bring them prosperity, but if they deserted him the consequences would be devastation." [Karen Armstrong; *A History of God*, page 53]

Predictably, the Islamic tradition keys into the same falsehood, by seemingly unifying the group of ruling gods of the world into one false Almighty, Jehovah/Allah. Quran 17: 111 reads, "And say: Praise be to Allah, Who hath not taken unto Himself a son, and **Who hath no partner in the Sovereignty**, nor hath He any protecting friend through dependence." The Quran even makes it an unforgivable sin to say that Jehovah/Allah has partners. Quran 4:48 reads, "Lo! Allah forgiveth not that a partner should be ascribed unto Him. ... Whoso ascribeth partners to Allah, he hath indeed invented a tremendous sin."

It should be noted however, that the actual entity that appeared to Muhammad on top of Mount Hira in AD 610 on that fateful seventeenth night of Ramadan was "archangel" Gabriel and not Allah. It is important to know too that the entire Quran was personally dictated to Muhammad by "archangel" Gabriel and not Allah.

At some point in the Quranic dictation, "archangel" Gabriel even found it necessary to dictate verses to clarify the issue of Jehovah/Allah's perceived supremacy over the "highest chiefs." He made it explicit that Jehovah/Allah is just an individual member of the "highest chiefs" that rule the world of humans, and that he has his own specific role and obligations. The *"most high"* gods merely regard and respect him as the ceremonial "**Possessor of the highest rank**." [Quran 40:15 Iranian Translation]

Gabriel said: "There is not one of Us but [each one of Us] hath his own known position. Lo! We, even We are they who set the ranks. Lo! We, even We are they who [had decided to] hymn His [Allah's] praise. ... [We are] the Highest Chiefs." [Quran 37:164-166, 8] But even with the well-documented evidence to the contrary, Muslims still hold that Jehovah/Allah has no partners, as Quran 112 in conclusion, still insists that Allah is the only "One."

Anyway, the New Revised Standard Version (NRSV) footnote on Deuteronomy 32:8 reads, "Gods, the divine beings who belong to the heavenly court (see Gen 1: 26n). To these heavenly beings, Jehovah delegated authority to govern other nations, but Israel was claimed as **Jehovah's own portion**. Deut 32: 11-12; Ex 19: 4." Thus, the footnote clearly captures the true status of the "gods" with whom Jehovah/Allah shared out the territories and peoples of the newly created world order 'in the beginning.' They jointly make up the wicked principalities that hold ignorant humans as captives on planet Earth.

Sadly enough, the Jews, customary Christians, and Muslims adamantly call their religions "monotheism," while in fact, they practice "monolatry"—the worship of only one god where several others are believed to exist. But although the three so-called monotheistic religions of the world have rhetorically transformed Jehovah/Allah into the sole creator of the entire universe, they have not successfully made him the sole ruler of our present earthly world. The Scripture still makes it clear that he and his "Let Us" partners partitioned the earth and its peoples into autonomous kingdoms or principalities, with each ruling over his own *allotted* share.

So, Jehovah/Allah is simply a king among the other equal ranking kings of the earthly world. The Bible talks of the *kingdoms* of the world because where there are kings there are kingdoms. There are eight mystical kingdoms in all and eight such false kings of the world. Revelation 17:11(NLT) reads: "[Jehovah/Allah], the scarlet beast that was [once a living spirit], but is no longer, is the eighth king [of the earthly kingdoms]. He is like the other seven, and he, too, is headed for [self-]destruction."

Jehovah/Allah himself had personally assured the Israelites that theirs had been the only family of people he ever knew on earth, and that Jerusalem had been his eternal dwelling place.

Other families of the earth belong to the other gods of the earth. "You only have I known **of all the families of the earth**; ... "You are my [only] witness," he said to them, "and my servant **whom I have chosen**, that you may know and believe me and understand that I am He. ... "And you shall say to Pharaoh, 'Thus says Jehovah, **Israel is my first-born son**, and I say to you "Let my son go that he may serve me;" if you refuse to let him go, behold, **I will slay your [own] firstborn son**.'" ... And "Jehovah has taken you, and brought you forth of the iron furnace, out of Egypt, to be a people for his own possession, as at this day." ... "O children of Israel! Remember My favor wherewith I favored you and how **I preferred you to (all) creatures**. [Amos 3:2; Isaiah 43:10; Exodus 4:22; Deuteronomy 4:20; Quran 2:47]

It was obvious from the actual circumstances surrounding the Jewish Exodus that Jehovah was not really contending with the human Pharaoh of Egypt, but against the tutelary god and king of the territorial kingdom of Egypt. Portraying himself as the **bigger snake** that swallowed the **smaller snake of Egypt** was a clear statement to that effect. Otherwise, his murderous escapades and arrogant show of brutal strength against innocent Egyptians were totally senseless and unwarranted. Battle against the mystical god and king of Egypt was one of his protracted cryptic battles against the other gods and kings of the world as he struggled to make them "give over their powers" to him for a unified opposition against the expected Messiah of their common human slaves.

These facts are made clearer by Moses' personal testimonies. Once, he asked the battered Jewish Exodus in Deuteronomy 4:34, "has **any god** ever attempted to go and take a nation for himself **from the midst of another nation**, by trials, by signs, by wonders, and by war, by a mighty hand and an outstretched arm, and by great terrors, according to all that Jehovah your God did for you in Egypt before your eyes?" And in Deuteronomy 3:21-22 he said to them, "You have seen for yourself everything Jehovah your God has

done to these two kings. He **will do the same to all the kingdoms** on the west side of the Jordan."

So, whether so-called monotheists accept it or not, our earthly world is made up of autonomous mystical kingdoms ruled over by autonomous mystical kings of whom Jehovah/Allah is but one. This proves that the mystical rulership of the world is indeed the joint enterprise of equal ranking accomplices.

The fact that the world was invented within the Outer Darkness by entities groping within darkness explains why the creation is grossly imperfect. This fact should be sufficient to prove to any clear-thinking human being that our perfect heavenly Father was neither the creator nor a co-ruler of the world. Of course, the Scripture says so clearly. 1 John 2:16 reads: "For all that is in the world, the lust of the flesh and the lust of the eyes and the pride of life, is not of the Father but is of the world."

Was it not surprising that the ruling kings of the federated kingdoms of the world nominated "the Devil" to tempt and *deliver* all the "authority and glory" of their joint dream world to Jesus Christ who they all considered an archenemy? Luke 4:5-6 reads: "And the devil took him [Jesus Christ] up, and showed him all the kingdoms of the world in a moment of time, and said to him, 'To you I will give all this authority and their glory; for it has been *delivered* to me [by mutual consensus], and I give it to whom I will."

That seemingly unimportant stunt proved that Jehovah/Allah was indeed "the Beast," "the Devil," and "the Spokesman" of the other kings of the world. As Revelations 17:13 says, "These are of one mind and give over their power and authority to the beast; [that] they will make war on [Jesus Christ] the Lamb." Of course, the tempter was only being sarcastic because they all knew that Jesus Christ come into the world to work against their devilish interests.

Nominating "the Devil" to tempt Jesus Christ on their behalf proved the fact that the Devil is the principal ruler of the world.

But the Devil can only be the spokesperson of a group of devils. It also showed the true integrity of the so-called kings of the world. Well, Jesus Christ rejected their dubious pact outrightly, thereby proving beyond doubt that neither he nor his Father had any part in both the making and the day-to-day rulership of the world. Indeed, the Messiah stated clearly that he was not in league with Jehovah/Allah and the ruling kings of the world. "I am not of this world," he said. [John 8:23]

Finally, the Father is the only true King in existence and his glorious heavenly Kingdom is only one. The so-called kingdoms of the world are imaginary, and the so-called kings of the world are overambitious fallen dead spirits pretending to be what they know they are not and can never become. Of course, falsehood, greed and hierarchy spirit are the hallmarks of false life of the world. Some entities try to outwit others, sometimes by merely assuming bogus names that ordinarily tend to set them apart as more important or mightier than the rest. This is why Jehovah/Allah goes by numerous false titles and epithets, and his faceless accomplices call themselves *arch*angels, implying that they are something bigger than angels.

Jehovah/Allah does not only call himself the God "Most High," but also blindly argues that besides him there is no other god. How can he be the "Most High God" when there are no other gods, who are perhaps lower than him? That shows how mentally suffocated these overambitious fallen dead spirits are.

Muslims ritually chant "Allahu Akbar" in their everyday prayers and as a general declaration of faith and thanksgiving. It literally means "Allah is Greater!" But they do not know or say who he is greater than. It could mean that Allah is greater than the humans or perhaps, greater than the universe. It really makes no sense.

The truth is that there is only one type of beings in the entire universe—fallen dead spirits! The Scripture says that "This world is a dark place, and its people [all the inhabiting spirits] have no light." [2 Esdras 14:20 (GNB)] So, no spirit is greater or lesser in the world since all are equally restricted in the Outer Darkness. Jehovah/Allah, the so-called archangels, jinn, humans and all other mortal lifeforms in the universe are fallen dead spirits and nothing more. None can truly be considered superior, wiser, or greater among a group of people groping in total darkness. The same goes for a group of people drowning in a deep dark bottomless ocean.

In fact, the Quran makes it clear that the only person who will be deemed successful in this world is the one who worked conscientiously and regained spiritual perfection. Quran 91:7-10 reads: "And a spirit and Him [the Father] who perfected it and inspired it (with conscience of) what is wrong for it and (what is) right for it. **He is indeed successful who causeth it [his spirit] to grow**, and he is indeed a failure who stunteth it." Obviously, Jehovah/Allah is the most stunted spirit in the world. He does not only reject spiritual regeneration for himself, but he also prevents others from working conscientiously to attain spiritual perfection.

In fact, Jesus Christ says that we are all brethren in the world. People should respect and love one another but none should be regarded as father, god, master, teacher, superior or greater than any other. "But you are not to be called rabbi, for you have one **teacher, and you are all brethren**," he says. "And call no man your father on earth, for you have one Father, who is in heaven. Neither be called masters, for you have one master, the Christ. **He who is greatest among you shall be your servant**; whoever exalts himself will be humbled, and whoever humbles himself will be exalted." [Matthew 23:8-12] This is the gospel truth in a nutshell!

THE UNCHANGED WILL OF THE FATHER FOR HIS FALLEN DEAD SONS IN THE WORLD

I am sure that information garnered from Ezekiel 18:20, Jude 6 and Genesis 1:1-2 in the preceding subheading have helped us to understand the true origin of our present world of darkness. We have seen that the realm of perfect Light and the realm of perfect Darkness exist eternally as direct opposite aspects of the Father who is eternal Origin of entire existence. The two realms are eternally separated in the Father by an inviolable chasm and designated for different divine purposes in accordance with his overall Divine Design.

We have also seen that the finite universal eruption triggered within the realm of perfect Darkness by corrupt fallen spirits represents an aberration, as it violates the Father's eternal Devine Design. And despite the presence of artificial lights of the stars, the finite universe remains lifeless, dark and *empty* because it is completely devoid of Divine Light and divine activities. It also remains chaotic, precarious, and imperfect because it was wrought in darkness by corrupt spirits.

The realm of perfect Light is the eternal domain of the Father and the realm of his positive influence. Perfect spirits who abide by the eternal norm of perfection dwell in absolute bliss in his presence and are in perfect harmony with his divine will. They have eternal life and are unlimited in their perfect capabilities and creative activities. They freely create perfect worlds and universes within the infinite realm of positive expressions. That is why Jesus Christ says, "There is more than enough room in my Father's home." [John 14:2(NLT)]

The realm of perfect Darkness, on the other hand, is the realm of the Father's negative influence. What that means is that the realm is not designated for any aspect of *positive* existence. Because it is devoid of Divine Light, it cannot support true life and perfect creative activities. Any action or activity that disturbs the eternal order and tranquility of the perfect divine reserve is not in tune with the Father's Divine Design and therefore, would be characterized by *negative* aspects of perfection.

That is why indelible darkness and imperfection define false existence in our finite chaotic universe. But imperfection and evilness speak of the true nature of the imperfect spirits that invented the shambolic universe within the eternal divine reserve and not of the infinite realm of perfect Darkness. That is why the Scripture speaks of "redemption" for the fallen dead sons of the Father that are trapped within the Outer Darkness. And that is why Jesus Christ says, concerning our present worldly existence, "Every plant which my heavenly Father has not planted will be rooted up." [Matthew 15:13]

Some may be inclined to imagine that perfect spirits and imperfect spirits existed eternally in their disparate realms. If that were the case, we would not be here talking about spiritual redemption, salvation, resurrection and reunion with the Father. We would not be hoping for the ultimate spiritual exodus back to the *proper* abode of our fallen dead spirits.

Even going strictly by the authoritative Scriptural information at our disposal, we can already see clearly that true "eternal life" does not exist anywhere within any sphere of our dying universe. Artificial cyclic process of life and death experienced by mortal beings on planet Earth, for instance, is on the negative aspect of perfection. Indeed, true eternal life is a positive aspect of the Father and belongs only to the spiritual realm of perfect Light. In fact, the Father is Light and Life himself and he dwells in the realm of Light. He is the eternal Tree of Life and only the perfect spirits who dwell within his positive influence have true eternal life.

All perfect spirits within the perfect heavenly Kingdom of the Father are divinely endowed with the right of choice between two eternal destinies and that choice entails permanent affirmation. Free will is a core aspect of the heavenly norm of perfection and it applies *only* to perfect spirits within the realm of perfect existence. The precept, "the spirit that sins shall die," permanently offers a choice between two extreme eternal destinies to every perfect spirit. He must continuously choose between continuing to dwell in perfection as a living spirit or sinking into eternal perdition in the Outer Darkness as fallen dead spirit.

"Sin," in the case of the living spirits, is the simple act of desiring and opting for eternal detachment from the perfect heavenly household of the Father. And "death" means detachment from the eternal Source of divine life. Since the Father is the Tree of perfect eternal Life, no spirit can possibly live without him. True free will, therefore, indicates that all perfect spirits have clear knowledge of the difference between life and death, right and wrong and good and evil. The Father does not hide from them the facts that true eternal life is impossible in the Outer Darkness or that spiritual death is eternal.

The norm of perfection applies equally to the Father as it does to the least of the living spirits within his heavenly household. The Father himself knows the eternal consequences of misuse of divine free will and thus maintains his unsullied nature and *proper* position forever. That is why the Scripture says that "the Father cannot be tempted with evil and he himself tempts no one." [James 1:13]

Absolute free will means exactly what it says but *only* in the realm of perfect existence. Fallen dead spirits in the Outer Darkness thrive on lawlessness. They exist without any binding precepts, and no one possesses the power of making free choices without being constrained by external forces or influences. Thus, many find themselves addicted to various vices beyond their control even when they genuinely struggle to embrace goodness. That is why accepting the Father's offer of spiritual salvation by Jesus Christ is such a terminal battle for humans on planet Earth. It demands perseverance and continuous struggle against detracting external forces and influences.

It is important to clarify that the fallen dead spirits in the Outer Darkness did not necessarily sin against the Father, but against eternal heavenly order. Knowingly violating the eternal norm of perfection meant that they equally sinned against themselves because they were bona fide stakeholders in the heavenly household. The statement of genuine repentance by the proverbial prodigal son to his ever-loving father portrays this fact clearly. He said to himself, "I will arise and go to my father, and I will say to him, 'Father, I have **sinned against heaven and before you**; I am no longer worthy to be called your son.'" [Luke 15:18-19]

As stipulated by the eternal precept, the heavenly dropouts were instantly spewed out of their heavenly dwelling and rendered Fatherless, lifeless and utterly loveless in the Outer Darkness. Today, humans have plethora of calamitous experiences recorded in the annals of human history to prove that life without the Father indeed, means death. Humans ought to have become fully convinced that choosing to abandon our "proper dwelling place" in the Father's realm of perfect existence in favor of experimental life of sensual pleasure in the Outer Darkness was indeed painful and utterly foolish.

This is equally true for Jehovah/Allah and the so-called gods of our earthly world. We are all living in bondage to sin and the painful wages of it. And it should be clearly stated that we are being self-afflicted in the Fatherless world that we created for ourselves.

The excruciating sting of spiritual death is eternal for all fallen dead spirits in the Outer Darkness, as stipulated by the heavenly norm of perfection. So, our self-affliction ought to be eternal. But our loving heavenly Father graciously offers an undeserved "second chance" to all heavenly dropouts in the universe. To that effect, Jesus Christ says, "it is not my heavenly Father's will that even one of these little ones should perish." [Matthew 18:14(NLT)] Hence, the Father sent us the heavenly Christ to rekindle and resurrect all fallen dead spirits who would willingly choose spiritual rebirth over eternal self-damnation in the Outer Darkness.

Jesus Christ affirms the Father's will, saying, "For this is the will of my Father, that everyone who sees the Son and believes in him should have [regain] eternal life; and I will raise him up at the last day." [John 6:40] Every true disciple of Jesus Christ testifies the power of love of our truly loving Father that draws us back from death to life through his Son. "And this is the testimony," says 1 John 5:11-12 "that the Father gave us eternal life, and this life is in his Son. He who has the Son has life; he who has not the Son of the Father has not life."

The infiniteness of the Father's love is indicated in his divine initiative and willingness to rescue and restore his fallen lost sons to their full spiritual heritage. His love manifests especially in his divine forbearance and perseverance in safely guiding them through the labyrinths of obstacles on their way back home. The **unchanged will of the Father is to rescue, to redeem,** and **to resurrect** his fallen dead sons from the eternal consequences of their fatal misjudgment.

The Father chose to rescue his lost sons out of absolute self-volition because love is natural to him. Therefore, there are words and actions that no right-thinking mind will knowingly attribute to the Father with respect to the issue of human salvation. Words like jealousy, jealous rage, wrath, vengeance against human beings, etc. cannot possibly come out of the Father's mouth. He cannot possibly be the self-seeking Jehovah/Allah that wields the blood-sated sword against defenseless humans on planet Earth, that terrorizes and slaughters people who would not bow before him as *God Almighty*, which he is not.

Well, the Scripture says that "The Father so loved the world [his fallen dead sons in the world] that he gave [sent] his only Son, that whoever believes in him should not perish but have [regain] eternal life." And it stresses the fact that "The Father sent the Son into the world, not to condemn the world, but that the world might be saved through him." [John 3:16-17]

John 3:16 is the most popular verse of the entire New Testament of the Bible with most customary Christian preachers. Bible commentators have said that "The entire Gospel comes to a focus in this verse." Martin Luther called this verse "**The Gospel in miniature.**" But how many of these church ministers really know the true meaning and full implications of this wonderful little verse? Yet, multitudes of laypeople rely completely on such ministers to explain to them the great mysteries of spiritual salvation by Jesus Christ, our Messiah.

Indeed, John 3:16 captures the everlasting nature of the Father's love, which motivated his plan of salvation for us in the first place. It also portrays the selfless love of the heavenly Christ who willingly stepped into our region of death to accomplish the Father's divine will. Jesus Christ died when he willingly stepped into our region of death just so that we might live. Hence, he says, "Greater love has no man than this, that a man lay down his life for his friends." [John 15:13] He also says, "The Father loves me because I sacrifice my life so I may take it back again. [No one forced me to do so] I sacrifice it voluntarily." [John 10:17-18(NLT)]

Therefore, John 3:16 lays sound foundation for a clearer understanding of the true mission of Jesus Christ in the world. The motivating factor in all this is perfect love. The Father is Love and he chose to manifest in his Son for the spiritual wellbeing of people who willfully forsook him. The Scripture says, "In this the love of the Father was made manifest among us, that the Father sent his **only Son** into the world, so that we might live [again] through him. In this is love, **not that we loved the Father but that he loved us** and sent his Son to be the expiation for our sins. ... We [are now learning to] love, because **he first loved us**." [1 John 4:9-10, 19]

Jesus Christ, our Messiah, epitomizes the Father's exemplary love for all fallen dead spirits in the world. If we eventually learn to love the Father again, it would be because he continued loving us despite our sins and has given us practical examples through his Son. And we can indeed love the Father again by practicing to truly respect and love our fellow human beings as we love ourselves.

I once listened to one of the major Pentecostal TV preachers in Nigeria explaining the meaning of John 3:16 to his national audience. He spoke so authoritatively that most of the people who listened to him would have automatically accepted everything he was saying without a second thought. However, I could easily see the deliberate loose thinking on his part. It was either he did not know the truth, or he was knowingly trying to mislead his viewers. He told his audience that "the world" that the Father so loved was the cosmos or the material superstructures of the world and not the fallen dead human spirits in the world.

He argued that *God* created the world perfect in the beginning, but that human beings destroyed it beyond repair, which made *God* very angry. He dramatically demonstrated the absolute nature of the sacrifice and effort that *God* exerted in designing and creating the world and concluded that *God* sent his Son into the world to restore his beautiful world that human beings have bastardized. He insisted that the verse held the hope of salvation, not for the entrapped human spirits in the world who are rather considered guilty of having caused *God* so much grief, but for the ramshackle material world itself.

Such calculated misinterpretation of the Scripture confirms the official status of customary Christianity as being "antichrist by default." Of course, human religion in general is the deadliest propaganda machinery in the hand of Jehovah/Allah and the self-seeking gods of the world. It exists to help the gods turn the truth on its head, and to return enlightened humanity to the Edenic stockade of ignorance. All worldly religions stand opposed to the Father's divine will in the world. They are expressly in business to make salvation difficult for captive human spirits, to lead as many of them as possible to the *second* eternal death at the close of the Father's dispensation of grace. True Christianity is not a religion but a way of life.

The truth is that all worldly religions worship Jehovah/Allah in different names either knowingly or unknowingly. He says to Muhammad, "Say (unto mankind): Cry unto Allah, or cry unto the Beneficent, **unto whichsoever ye cry (it is the same)**. His are the most beautiful names." [Quran 17:110] The most obvious examples are the three-sister Abrahamic religions. Jehovah/Allah is known as "YHWH" in Judaism, "Jehovah" in customary Christianity, and "Allah" in Islam. Yet, heavily beguiled adherents of the three religions hardly see or agree that they are worshiping the same master schemer.

Jehovah/Allah is a seasoned fraudster. He does not and has never meant well for human beings. He does not give a damn about the plight of human beings on earth or for the salvation of their captive spirits. In fact, he is the one who makes this life a living hell for human beings. And he works tirelessly to mislead captive human spirits, through his various misleading religious injunctions that instigate religious intolerance and senseless wars among ignorant humans. Of course, he makes his ultimate intent very clear in the Quran, saying, "Verily I shall fill hell with the jinn and mankind together." [Quran 11:119]

Jehovah/Allah only cares about how to sustain his oppressive regime over ignorant humans on planet Earth. His only concern is the survival or salvation of the worldly status quo that sustains his false earthly kingdom. It is not difficult to see therefore, that the Pentecostal TV preacher who interpreted John 3:16 to mean that the Father sent his Son to restore "the world" and not to redeem sinful human spirits was being inspired by Jehovah/Allah.

For obvious reasons, Jehovah/Allah is terminally opposed to the Father's divine arrangement that mandates Jesus Christ to rekindle and resurrect fallen dead human spirits whom he considers his perpetual slaves. He considers enlightened human beings to be his permanent enemies because, according to him, they are the ones who have destroyed his wonderful dream for the world. But his actual enemy ought to be the heavenly Christ who brought divine enlightenment to ignorant humans and works still to set their captive spirits free from his deadly hold. Nevertheless, he swore vengeance and utter destruction against vulnerable human beings because he lacks the power to oppose or confront the heavenly Christ directly.

Jehovah/Allah has remained disgruntled since his decisive defeat in Eden, and he speaks openly of his utter despair and grief. His lamentations, which are entirely laced in falsehood go like these:

- "Before I created this world or the people who would live in it, no one opposed me, because no one existed. When I had created the world, I supplied it with an abundance of food and a Law of profound wisdom, but the people I created lived corrupt lives. I looked at my world and saw that it was ruined. I saw that my earth was in danger of being destroyed by the wicked plans of the people who had come into it. When I saw this, I found it very difficult to spare them, ... **So let them perish**—all those people who were born only to be lost.

- "The people of this world used their reason and sinned [against me]; ... And that is why they will suffer torment.

- **"I will not be sad about the large number of people who will be lost**, because even now they last no longer than a vapor; they disappear like fire and smoke; they catch fire, blaze up, and quickly go out." [2 Esdras 9:18-22; 7:72, 61(GNB)]

Other verses of the Bible and the Quran also capture Jehovah/Allah's frustration, outbursts, powerlessness, and endless failures:

- "And Jehovah was sorry that he had made man on the earth, and **it grieved him** to his heart. So, Jehovah said, 'I will blot out man whom I have created from the face of the ground.'" [Genesis 6:6-7] He tried but failed woefully.

- "Behold, **the day of Jehovah comes, cruel, with wrath and fierce anger**, to make the earth a desolation and to destroy its sinners from it. ... "I will take vengeance, and I will spare no man." [Isaiah 13:9; 47:3] Indeed, Jehovah/Allah has relentlessly terrorized and brutalized defenseless humans, but he has not and will never prevail over enlightened humanity.

- "The day is the day of Jehovah God of hosts, **a day of vengeance**, to avenge himself on his [human] foes. The sword shall devour and be sated, and drink its fill of their blood." [Jeremiah 46:10] Again, Jehovah/Allah has slaughtered and ceaselessly fed on the innocent blood of men, women, and children since his humiliation in Eden, yet his grief remains.

- Finally, he swears, "Verily I shall fill hell with the [fallen dead spirits of] jinn and mankind together." [Quran 11:119]

These are unmistakable words of a frustrated evil spirit. It is evident from his bitter and defiant utterances that Jehovah/Allah is both Antichrist and anti-humanity. It is clear therefore, that he cannot possibly be the one who sent Jesus Christ into the world to redeem captive human spirits.

If the Pentecostal TV preacher were not an apostle of Jehovah/Allah, if he were not antichrist by default, he would have read John 3:16 objectively to capture the true context. The Father sent Jesus Christ into the world, "so that **everyone** [not the world] who believes in him may not die [the *second* spiritual death in the Outer Darkness] but have eternal life."

The unchanged will of the Father is made very explicit in the golden verse. It is **to redeem and to give eternal life** to fallen dead spirits who are entangled in the world and are held captive by overambitious evil spirits. Jesus Christ did not come to stop the ultimate death of the universe. The universe is a tree that the Father did not plant; it must be completely uprooted. The material superstructures of the finite expanding universe are irredeemably destined to die eternal death at the end of time.

Some people think that the universe as we know it now will last forever. But space-time continuum does not imply eternity. Eternity means absence of time; but once time is involved, there is bound to be an end. Space-time continuum is a process and since it has a beginning; it is bound to have an end. As the Scripture says, "The world [itself] passes away, and the lust of it, but he [any fallen dead spirit] who does the will of the Father abides forever." [1 John 2:17]

Indeed, the writer of the Gospel and Epistles of John uses the word "world" in ways that can mean the cosmos, the earth, the people on earth, most people, people opposed to the Father, or the human system that is opposed to the Father's purpose. And in many cases, he switches from one meaning to another without explanation. However, a seasoned preacher like the one mentioned above could have only made such mistake deliberately. The world is truly irredeemable. If he did not know that he ought to have at least seen or felt that the world is indeed dying, naturally.

Finally, it should not be forgotten that all fallen dead spirits in the world are self-condemned and self-afflicted. But the central theme of the Father's salvation plan for all of them remains ever unchanged. It is **to redeem and restore** them to their full spiritual heritage in perfection through the redemptive mission of the heavenly Christ. Hence, the Scripture makes it clear that "The

Father sent his Son into the world not to judge the world, but to save the world through him."

In fact, the Scripture says that "There is no judgment against anyone who believes in him [Jesus Christ]. But anyone who does not believe in him has already been judged for not believing in the Father's one and only Son. **And the judgment is based on this fact:** [that] the Father's light came into the world, but people loved the darkness more than the light, for their actions were evil." [John 3:17-19(NLT)]

CHAPTER TWO

THE DIVINE OFFICE OF JESUS CHRIST OUR MESSIAH

It is no longer in dispute that the Father sent the heavenly Christ into the world to **rekindle, redeem,** and **resurrect** all fallen dead spirits that would willingly accept his gracious offer of divine amnesty. But the Father is Divine Spirit and Divine Light, and he dwells eternally in the spiritual realm of perfect existence with the heavenly Christ and all perfect spirits. We know also that the Father's spiritual realm of Light is eternally separated by an unbridgeable chasm from the makeshift habitat of fallen dead spirits, which exists within the Outer Darkness.

So, we ought to expect that the heavenly Christ would utilize appropriate modes of communication in dealing with mortal human beings. During his *first* advent into the world, he interacted with Adam and Eve in Eden via divine inspiration as Spirit of Knowledge. They understood him perfectly and the Scripture confirms that "the eyes of both were opened, and they knew that they were naked; and they sewed fig leaves together and made themselves aprons [of moral rectitude]." [Genesis 3:7] He reiterated the Father's divine will to Adam and Eve, assuring them that "they will not surely die" as Jehovah/Allah had threatened.

He also assured them that he would return to the world in human form in due course amongst their posterity to speak directly to captive human beings in their own language. Then, he inspired Adam and his direct descendants as prophets to create awareness of his expected *second* coming. Thus, Adam became the first true prophet of the heavenly Christ in the world. Other bona fide sons of Adam became true prophets after him and continued to prophesy expected incarnation of the heavenly Christ till John the Baptist heralded his actual arrival.

The Scripture confirms that in its appointed time, the heavenly Christ indeed incarnated in the world as the Father's Word of Life amongst the descendants of Adam and Eve as promised. "So, the Word [of Life] became human and made his home among us," says John 1:14(NLT). He was full of unfailing love and faithfulness. And we have seen his glory, the glory of the Father's one and only Son." Heb 2:14-15(NLT) equally says, "Because the Father's children are human beings [now]—made of flesh and blood—the Son also became flesh and blood. For only as a human being could he die, and only by dying could he break the power of [Jehovah/Allah] the devil, who had [wields] the power of death. Only in this way could he set free all who have lived their lives as slaves to the fear of dying."

Mark 1:4-8 says that "John came, baptizing in the desert region and preaching a baptism of repentance for the forgiveness of sins. ... And this was his message: 'After me will come one more powerful than I, the thongs of whose sandals I am not worthy to stoop down and untie. I baptize you with water, but he will baptize you with the Holy Spirit.'" And after he had baptized the Incarnated Christ, he testified to his followers, saying, "You yourselves know how plainly I told you, 'I am not the Messiah. I am only here to prepare the way for him.' ... Therefore, I am filled with joy at his success. He must become greater and greater, and I must become less and less." [John 3:28-30(NLT)]

As we all know, the Jews are direct descendants of Adam and Eve. All the true prophets of the heavenly Christ were Jews. But so were the false prophets of Israel; they were abducted sons of Adam, possessed by Jehovah/Allah's evil spirit and specifically inspired with contradictory prophesies to muddle the divine messages mediated by the true prophets of the heavenly Christ. Thus, the foundation of Judaism as a religion was seriously marred by the conflicting prophesies and activities of the true and the false prophets of Israel.

The Jews failed to correctly identify the Messiah when he appeared amongst them because Jehovah/Allah held them completely enthralled with his false prophesies. Jehovah/Allah craftily worded his false prophesies to convince the Jews that he was their only true savior, while the heavenly Christ that would come would be merely a false prophet who would attempt to lead them to an unknown god. He even decreed to them, well in advance, why and how they must put him to death. "But any prophet who falsely claims to speak in my name or who speaks in the name of another god must die," he decreed for them. [Deuteronomy 18:20(NLT)]

Thus, the Jews were already prejudiced and deeply motivated against their coming true Messiah. They could not even incline themselves toward distinguishing between the prophesies of the true prophets of the heavenly Christ and those of the false prophets of Jehovah/Allah. As a result, they missed out on the time of their divine visitation, and that greatly jeopardized their prime position as the bona fide custodians of the divine mission of Jesus Christ in the world.

But while they sought opportunity to kill him, in accordance with Jehovah/Allah's homicidal injunction of Deuteronomy 18:20, Jesus Christ plainly said to them, "You are [being] of your father [Jehovah] the devil, and your will is to do your father's desires. He was a murderer from the beginning, and has nothing to do with the truth, because there is no truth in him. When he lies, he speaks according to his own nature, for he is a liar and the father of lies." [John 8:44]

Even to this today, the Jews are still enthralled by Jehovah/Allah's false promises, even when it has become dead obvious that he is just a fraudster. They still cling to him as their only true savior, even when their practical experiences of endless national calamities and torments in the hands of the same God prove that he is in fact, their archenemy. The whole truth now stares the Jews in the face, yet they still do not seem to see the difference. They still have not realized that Jesus Christ was indeed the true Messiah that the true prophets of Israel prophesied would incarnate amongst them.

True disciples of Jesus Christ know that the Jews will eventually see and accept 'the true light that enlightens every man' in the world. But in the meantime, Jesus Christ continues to say to them, "I tell you, you will not see me again, until you say, 'Blessed is he who comes in the name of the Father.'" [Matthew 23:39]

Every true disciple of Jesus Christ understands the unique position of the lost sons of Adam to the divine mission Jesus Christ in the world and prays fervently that they would soon realize that Jehovah has never been a **Savior** but a **Savage** to the Jews. He began by revealing to Abraham the evils he intended for his descendants even before they were born. He said to him, "Know of a surety that your descendants will be sojourners in a land that is not theirs, and will be slaves there, and they will be oppressed for four hundred years." [Genesis 15:13] So, the more than 400 years of programmed enslavement of the Jews in Egypt and their subsequent ill-fated Exodus were entirely premeditated and stage-managed by Jehovah/Allah to portray himself as a kind of savior to the Jews.

Even after oppressing and humiliating the lost sons of Adam in Egypt by proxy, he personally led them into the harsh wilderness of Sinai, and for a whole 40 years he continued to starve, torment, and horrify them till he eventually slaughtered all the people he purportedly saved from slavery in Egypt.

Jehovah/Allah did not even stop with the horrors and mass slaughter of the Jewish Exodus. He has continued to endlessly enslave, humiliate, terrorize, torment and massacre the Jews by deliberately putting them through unending wars, exiles, pogroms, expulsions, holocaust, bloody intifadas, organized worldwide anti-Semitism, ghastly terror attacks and threat of extermination by Islamic extremists. Jehovah/Allah has never been anything else other than a resident evil to the Jews.

How can any right-thinking human being consider Jehovah/Allah a true savior or a good shepherd? What kind of savior or shepherd endlessly leads his sheep into danger and abandons them to be torn in pieces and eaten by wild beasts? It is obvious that Jehovah/Allah is but a Thief and a Hireling, while Jesus Christ is the true 'Good Shepherd' sent to the Jews and the rest of humankind from our loving heavenly Father.

Jesus Christ explains that "The thief comes only to steal and kill and destroy;" ... and a hireling "sees the wolf coming and leaves the sheep and flees; and the wolf snatches them and scatters them. ... He flees because he is a hireling and cares nothing for the sheep." Then he says of himself, "I am the good shepherd. The good shepherd lays down his life for the sheep. ... "I came that they may have life, and have it abundantly." [John 10:10-14]

Well, it should be reiterated that the period that the heavenly Christ communicated to humans through his true prophets ended with John the Baptist. When he finally incarnated amongst the lost sons of Adam as a human being, he spoke their human language, thus bringing the period of the true prophets of Israel to a definite end. Every other prophet after John the Baptist, whether of Jewish or customary Christian extraction, is a false prophet of Jesus Christ.

Jesus Christ spoke directly with the lost sons of Adam. He ate their food, experienced their joys and their pains, celebrated and wept with them; he forgave their original sins, healed the sick, raised the dead, and carried out numerous works of love and mercy amongst them, yet they remained prejudiced. So, he said, "If I had not done among them the works which no one else did [which Jehovah never did], they would not have sin; but now they have seen and hated both me and my Father." [John 15:24]

The heavenly Christ specifically chose *only* 12 Apostles for his earthly ministry. And for more than three years, he dwelt bodily in their midst, walked about Jerusalem and its environs with them, and did all his miraculous works of love and true humanity in their presence. Being the heavenly Teacher, he taught his chosen Apostles absolute truths directly through simple homilies, parables, authoritative gospel of the Kingdom, and by personal examples.

As the Master of the true prophets, he openly debunked and abrogated some of the false prophesies of the Old Testament in the streets of Jehovah/Allah's evil city of Jerusalem. His words and actions informed, inspired, and instilled the courage of rock in his true apostles and disciples, prompting Simon Bar-Jona to openly declare that Jesus was indeed "the Messiah, the Son of the living Father." [Matthew 16:16(NLT)]

Thus, Jesus Christ groomed and encouraged his true apostles and disciples to follow in his exact footsteps. He said to them, "You call me 'Teacher' and 'Lord,' and you are right, because that's what I am. ... I have given you an example to follow. Do as I have done to you." ... "So now I am giving you a new commandment: Love each other. Just as I have loved you, you should love each other. Your love for one another will prove to the world that you are my disciples." [John 13:13-15; 34-35(NLT)]

Sadly, Jehovah/Allah had already hatched and prophesied an evil plot against the Messiah and his true apostles and disciples well in advance. Zechariah 13:7-9 details how he planned to persecute and kill the Messiah, how he would infiltrate and scatter his true apostles and disciples, how he would kill two thirds of them and re-brainwash the remaining one third, and ultimately how he would steal away and falsify Christ's true gospel to the world. Zechariah 13:7-9 reads:

> "Awake, O sword, against my shepherd, against the man who stands next [opposed] to me," says Jehovah of hosts. "Strike the shepherd, that the sheep may be scattered; I [Jehovah] will turn my hand against the little ones. In the whole land, says Jehovah, two thirds shall be cut off and perish, and one third shall be left alive. And I [Jehovah] will

put this third into the fire, and refine them as one refines silver, and test them as gold is tested. [By the time I finish with the remaining one third,] They will call on my name, and I will answer them. I will say, 'They are my people'; and they will say, 'Jehovah is my God.'"

Being thorough in evil deeds, Jehovah/Allah executed his evil agendas against Jesus Christ to the letter. He crucified humankind's Messiah, persecuted and murdered two thirds of his true apostles, and re-indoctrinated the remaining one third. Next, he infiltrated the ranks of Christ's true apostles and disciples with his own false apostles, prophets and church fathers and ultimately stole away and falsified the true gospel of the heavenly Christ.

He personally founded customary Christianity through his own zealous apostle, Paul, who cunningly whisked away Christ's true gospel of the Kingdom from its true Jewish custodians and delivered it to pure Devil worshippers in Rome. Then, the so-called church fathers buried the true gospel of our heavenly Messiah in the catacombs of Jehovah/Allah's Church in Rome and floated a thoroughly falsified version that worships Jehovah/Allah as *God Almighty* in the world. Not surprisingly, customary Christians today, worship the murderous Jehovah in their hearts, while merely saying "in the name of Jesus Christ" with their lips.

Rather than following the very words of Jesus Christ whom it acknowledged to be the true Messiah, customary Christianity keyed directly into Jehovah/Allah's false prophesies and ordinances and became merely an extension of Judaism. Customary Christianity became the religion of false apostles, false prophets, false fathers, false teachers, antichrists and multitudes of beguiled laity.

The false operatives of the universal Church of Jehovah/Allah are thieves and hirelings, yet they are the sap of present customary Christianity. They are paid agents of the dreadful Antichrist and archenemy of true humanity, and they knowingly serve his will in return for monetary and material rewards. Meanwhile, they tirelessly steer ignorant churchgoers back to Jehovah/Allah's obnoxious Old Testament laws and injunctions, which Jesus Christ openly debunked and abrogated in the streets of Jerusalem.

Present customary Christianity is antichrist by default, obviously because it is a full-fledged institution of the world. Church leadership is hard wired to serve the will of Jehovah/Allah, the archenemy of true humanity, and the system is irreformable. Leaders of the Church, from the Vatican to the remotest village church in Africa, are mostly interested in money and worldly éclat. They dutifully preach financial and material *breakthroughs* and *prosperity* in the world despite Christ's express injunction against pursuit of material riches. They do so because they belong to the world and not to Jesus Christ.

Nevertheless, there are multitudes of churchgoers who truly love and desire the spiritual salvation of Jesus Christ. They go to church because they sincerely think that the church is all about Jesus Christ, and that Jesus Christ dwells in the churches. And though they feel deep in themselves that somethings are terribly wrong with the foundation and basic orientation of customary Christianity, they decide to focus on the love of Jesus Christ, knowing that he sees their hearts. Of course, Jesus Christ knows and sees the hearts of people who belong to him, and he protects them wherever they are at the present.

But it is not wise to sit comfortably in the company of people who knowingly work for your deadliest enemy. The Church was instituted for Jehovah witnessing; true disciples of Jesus Christ do not belong to customary Christianity. This may sound too drastic, but it is the gospel truth. So, it is both wise and safe to find out the truth and live by it, even if it means stepping off the bandwagon.

Jesus Christ says that "you will know the truth, and the truth will set you free." [John 8:32(NLT)] That may sound very easy, but it is not. The battle for spiritual salvation is indeed a matter of life and death. It is better therefore, to know and live by the truth than to merely believe and live by blind faith.

True disciples of Jesus Christ know that the Father is Divine Spirit. They know also that the resurrected Christ is perfect Spirit. So, neither the Father nor the heavenly Christ dwells in man-made tabernacles, temples, cathedrals, and mosques. Jehovah/Allah does because he is both a fallen dead spirit and a human.

For true disciples of Jesus Christ, the true church exists in their hearts. That is where the Father, the heavenly Christ and the Holy Spirit of truth dwell. Jesus Christ says so clearly. "In that day you will know that I am in my Father, and you in me, **and I in you**," he says ... "even the Spirit of truth, whom the world cannot receive, because it neither sees him nor knows him; you know him, for **he dwells with you**, and **will be in you**." [John 14:20,17]

Jesus Christ spoke about the present state of customary Christianity with the parable of the good seeds and the weeds. He said, "The kingdom of heaven may be compared to a man who sowed good seed in his field; but while men were sleeping, his enemy came and sowed weeds among the wheat and went away. So, when the plants came up and bore grain, then the weeds appeared also." [Matthew 13:24-26] The good seeds sowed by Jesus Christ were the flock of his true apostles and disciples, but following his crucifixion and ascension, Jehovah/Allah infiltrated the flock and sowed his own evil weeds amongst them, and customary Christianity became the outcome.

Beginning with Saul of Tarsus who stole the true gospel of Jesus from its true Jewish custodians and handed it over to well-known Devil worshippers in Rome, the weeds in present customary Christianity include the pope who they blasphemously also call *Holy Father*, the so-called church fathers, cardinals, archbishops, bishops, apostles, prophets, priests, deacons and the endless other church officers that notoriously parade themselves as *Men and Women of God*. They are all weeds within the true flock of the heavenly Christ. Their characters and preachments show clearly that they are antichrists.

In the first place, Jesus Christ clearly instructed that his true disciples should **"give to Caesar what belongs to Caesar, and give to the Father what belongs to the Father."** [Matthew 22:21(NLT)] To true disciples of Jesus Christ, the Father is the highest authority in every matter pertaining to the gospel of Jesus Christ, to safety and life, while emperor Caesar stood as the highest arbiter in worldly matters.

In strict obedience to his words, all true apostle of Jesus Christ stood firmly in professing his gospel of the Kingdom even at the point of death. Disciple Stephen continued to *appeal* to the highest office of the Father and the heavenly Christ as men like Saul and his disciples stoned him to death. "Lord Jesus, receive my spirit." ... "Lord, don't charge them with this sin!" were his prayers before he died. [Acts 7:59-60(NLT)] But Paul appealed to the highest court of Caesar in Rome when he was confronted with an issue that pertained exclusively to the defense of the gospel of Jesus Christ in Jerusalem. "I appeal to Caesar," he said to governor Porcius Festus without hesitation. [Acts 25:11]

Again, Jesus Christ clearly instructed that his true disciples should not call anyone or be called father, rabbi or master on earth because they are all equal as brothers and sisters in his flock. Matthew 23:8-12 captures the exact words and divine will of Jesus Christ our Messiah on this issue. It reads:

> "But you are not to be called rabbi, for you have one teacher, and you are all brethren. And call no man your father on earth, for you have one Father, who is in heaven. Neither be called masters, for you have one master, the Christ. He who is greatest among you shall be your servant; whoever exalts himself will be humbled, and whoever humbles himself will be exalted."

Jesus Christ was explicit on this issue, but Paul would not have that, because he was a weed planted by Jehovah/Allah among the true flock of the heavenly Christ, because he was a false apostle of Jesus Christ. Paul did not only call himself 'father,' thereby brazenly countering the solemn injunction of Jesus Christ, but he even urged beguiled churchgoers to imitate him and not Jesus Christ. His words read, "For though you have countless guides in Christ, you do not have many fathers. For **I became your father in Christ Jesus through the gospel.** I urge you, then, **be imitators of me.**" [1 Corinthians 4:15-16]

Thus, Paul exalted himself not only above all customary Christians but even above the Messiah himself. So, he will eventually be humbled, even as the Messiah had said. Paul must eventually be uprooted along with all the celebrated weeds of present subverted Christianity. True Christianity will reemerge at its appointed time, even as Jesus Christ assures his true flock.

When asked if his true disciples should immediately uproot the weeds from amongst their midst, Jesus Christ answered, 'No; lest in gathering the weeds you root up the wheat along with them. Let both grow together **until the harvest**; and at harvest time I will tell the reapers, Gather the weeds first and bind them in bundles to be burned, but gather the wheat into my barn.'" [Matthew 13:29-30]

The Father had purposely allowed ample time for the weeds to grow freely amongst the good seeds. Peradventure many will learn true repentance from the true flock of Jesus Christ. That is why the Scripture says that "many are called" even though it is known that "few would be chosen." It may even seem today that the weeds have completely suffocated the good seeds in customary Christianity. But, the Messiah already assured us that none of them would be lost in the end. "Those the Father has given me will come to me," he says. ... And this is the will of the Father, that I should not lose even one of all those he has given me, but that I should raise them up at the last day." [John 6:37-39(NLT)]

The time for true disciples of Jesus Christ to knowingly separate themselves from the weeds of customary Christianity is now. *The Final Testaments* heralds the expected *harvest time*, and it is already in progress. In reminding the true disciples of Jesus Christ that we are temples of the Living Father, the Scripture asks, "What harmony can there be between Christ and the Devil? ... And what union can there be between the Father's temple and idols? For we are the temple of the living Father." [2 Corinthians 6:15-16(NLT)]

Even though Jehovah's evil scheme against the Messiah and his true flock had seemed firm to him in the beginning, he soon realized that it was not quite foolproof after all. Although he successfully crucified the Messiah, persecuted and murdered two third of his true apostles, and even recolonized the remaining one third as planned, his problems rather became bigger.

It soon dawned on him that he would never be able to obtain total blind surrender to his devilish will from both Judaism and customary Christianity as presently constituted. He needed a new religion that lacked knowledge, reason, and common sense; a new religion of blind believers that would unconditionally surrender their spirits to his murderous "will and guidance." In fact, he lamented that Jews and customary Christians deviated from his cause because of the knowledge they received from Jesus Christ.

Of course, Jehovah had suspected that crucifying and running Jesus the Son of man out of his world may not permanently solve his problems. Somehow, he had the premonition well in advance that the Jews may never completely go along with him after seeing and hearing directly from the coming Messiah. So, he also prophesied his **"Plan C"** through his *false* prophets of Israel.

As the mouthpiece of Jehovah/Allah, Moses prophesied to the Jews, saying, "Jehovah your God will raise up for you a prophet like me from among you, **from your** [Ishmaelite] **brethren** - him you shall heed." [Deuteronomy 18:15] Jehovah also prophesied through Ezra about him eventually moving to a "new chosen people." He said to him: "Announce to my new people [the Ishmaelites] that I will give them the kingdom of Jerusalem, which I had planned to give to Israel." [2 Esdras 2:10(GNB)]

Accordingly, Jehovah/Allah quickly founded Islam in AD 610 through Muhammad, the Ishmaelite brethren of the Jews, and dramatically handed over his Temple Mount in Jerusalem to Muslims. Islam became Jehovah/Allah's *final* reactive force against the redemptive mission of the heavenly Christ in the world. Islam was to serve both as a damage control measure to the redemptive effects of Christ-consciousness in the world and as a ruthless counterattack on true humanity.

Thus, with Islam, Jehovah/Allah radically redefined religion to reflect the severity of his *final* battles against the redemptive mission of the heavenly Christ in the world, while demanding nothing but "total blind *surrender*," from his ignorant devotees. He says, "Lo! religion with Allah (is) **The Surrender** (to His will and guidance). Those who (formerly) received the Scripture [Jews and Christians] differed [deviated] only after knowledge came unto them [from Jesus Christ]." [Quran 3:19]

Straightaway, Islam demands hatred of 'knowledge, reason and common sense' from Muslims, which is why all radical Islamic groups in the world are terminally opposed to Judeo-Christian education and moral value systems. One Islamic extremist group in Nigeria even openly call itself "Boko Haram," meaning "Western education and social virtues are forbidden."

But hatred of 'knowledge, reason and common sense' has only produced death cults of Islamic barbarians all over the world who are unreasoning, brutal, adamant, suicidal, and genocidal. While they enjoy slaughtering people of other religious faith in most gruesome ways who they term *infidels*, they celebrate and worship their own dead fellow murderers as *martyrs* who have merely proceeded to paradise to be rewarded by Allah. That is so insane!

Enlightened human beings know that slavery is bondage, yet footnote to Quran 43:59 in *The meaning of The Glorious Quran by*

Marmaduke Pickthall claims that being a slave to Allah is the proudest designation every Muslim desires. The footnote reads:

> 'Abd Allah', "slave of Allah," is a proud designation with the Muslims, bondage to Allah implying liberation from all earthly servitude.

This is utter ignorance because Allah is, in fact, the Lord of "all earthly servitude." Anyway, Islam represents advanced system of mental hypnosis on the sons of Ishmael by Jehovah/Allah whose basic spell had failed to work as desired on their Jewish brethren. Jehovah/Allah was forced to tighten his wicked grip on the helpless sons of Ishmael by instilling extreme fear of him in them to avoid losing them to the heavenly Christ as he did the Jews and Christians.

So, speaking of the strangling hold that Jehovah/Allah has on all Muslims, Quran 39:16 says, "They have an awning of fire above them and beneath them a dais (of fire). With this doth Allah appall [horrify] His bondmen. O **My bondmen, therefor fear Me!**" Quran 58:22 then says, "Thou wilt not find folk who believe in Allah and the Last Day loving those who oppose Allah and His messenger: even though they be their fathers or, their sons or their brethren or their clan. As for such, He hath written [blind] faith upon their hearts and hath strengthened them with a [bloodthirsty] Spirit from Him, ... Allah is well pleased with them, and they are well pleased with Him. **They are Allah's party.**"

As we have seen, Islam thrives on irrational fear, blind faith and falsehood. And in synch with Jehovah/Allah's old gambits of outright lies, false prophesies, and distortion of facts, Islam opened with smear campaign against the true nature and mission of Jesus Christ. The sole intent of Islamic propaganda machinery was to reduce Jesus Christ to an inconsequential religious figure, while fanatically promoting Muhammad of Arabia as the ultimate of all prophets of the world.

Accordingly, although the Quran recognizes Jesus Christ as humankind's heavenly Messiah, Islamic tradition hold that he was merely a prophet and messenger amongst so many that Jehovah/Allah had sent into the world. In fact, Muslims regard Jesus Christ as a renegade prophet of Jehovah/Allah and a messiah without a definite portfolio.

Quran 10:47 says that "for every nation there is a messenger," meaning that Jehovah/Allah had sent prophets or messengers to every tribe of peoples on the face of the earth to propagate his futile cause. In fact, Islamic tradition claims that there had been 124,000 of such prophets, messengers, or *reformers* of the earthly order, from Adam to Muhammad. Expectedly, these included well-known Jewish prophets, great sages of old, gurus, and outstanding religious and military world rulers.

This information perfectly captures the unending and fruitless efforts by the fallen dead gods of the world to evolve a workable earthly order. Nevertheless, it also presupposes that Jehovah/Allah is absolutely in charge of the earthly situation and that the divine office of the heavenly Christ does not transcend and threaten his paramount authority. But we know that that is not the case at all. Divine mission of Jesus Christ in the world has been a nightmare for Jehovah/Allah since his humiliating defeat in Eden that put an end to his Edenic daydream forever. That is why he has been humping from one religion to another and relying entirely on falsehood and religious propaganda to stay relevant among uninformed humans.

So, while Islamic tradition concedes that Jesus Christ was indeed the **one and only expected Messiah** of humankind, it still argues that he was one of the 124,000 automata that Jehovah/Allah sent to the world. Yet the Quran states clearly that Jesus Christ is of the *Righteous God* and that he is uniquely *illustrious in the world and in the Hereafter*. Neither Muhammad nor any of the 124,000 messengers of Jehovah/Allah was ever ascribed with such honor and divine nature. Quran 3:45-46 reads: "O Mary! Lo! Allah giveth thee glad tidings of a word from Him, **whose name is the Messiah**, Jesus, son of Mary, **illustrious in the world and in the Hereafter**, ... and **he is of the Righteous**."

Yet, in a desperate attempt to trivialize the divine nature of Jesus Christ that Islamic tradition already acknowledged, Quran 4:171 proceeded to argue that Jews and Christians were only exaggerating the uniqueness of the heavenly Christ: "O People of the Scripture [Jews and Christians]! Do not exaggerate in your religion nor utter aught concerning Allah save the truth. **The Messiah, Jesus son of Mary**, *was only a messenger of Allah*, and *His word which He conveyed unto Mary*, and *a spirit from Him*. ... Allah is only One God. Far is it removed from His transcendent majesty that he should have a son."

The Quran makes it explicit that Jesus Christ, the Messiah, is not the son of Jehovah/Allah. And that is very correct. In fact, Quran 112:3 says plainly that Allah "begetteth not." Jehovah/Allah is Enslaver of vulnerable spirits; he is the Captor, and human spirits are his captives. He personally says repeatedly in the Quran that humans are merely his bondmen and bondwomen. Hence, Jesus Christ calls him "thief and robber" of spirits who "comes only to steal and kill and destroy." [John 10:10] Muslims do not dispute these facts. What they refuse to accept is that Jesus Christ, the Messiah, is the Son of the Living Divine Spirit who indeed "begetteth" all spirits in existence.

Paradoxically, Muslims believe Quran 4:171, which says that "Allah is only One God" and that "the Messiah, Jesus son of Mary" is a "Word" and a "Spirit" from Allah, and yet they vehemently argue that Jesus Christ is not the son of "God." But saying that Jesus Christ is a "Word" or "Spirit" from Jehovah/Allah is the same as saying that he emanated from Allah, that he is in fact, Allah's son.

Well, Muslims lack the basic wisdom to deal with this kind of cover-up; they simply say whatever Allah tells them to say but do not really believe it. Acknowledging that being a "Word" or

"Spirit" from Allah makes Jesus Christ a son of Allah would have busted the bigger lie that they seek to uphold. Anyway, that would have been preposterous and blasphemous. What this means is that the Muslims are subconsciously aware that Jehovah/Allah is not God. But Islam is inherently devoid of 'knowledge, reason and common sense.'

Jehovah/Allah and Jesus Christ, the Messiah, are strictly opposite in every respect. The heavenly Christ is a living Spirit, while Jehovah/Allah is a fallen dead spirit. Jesus Christ is the Son of our *Living* heavenly Father who dwells eternally in the transcendent realm of Light and perfect existence. Besides, a dead spirit does not beget a living spirit. It is remarkable that Jehovah/Allah himself could not help conceding the fact that Jesus Christ is the **"Righteous Messiah** of the World." It is also remarkable that none of Jehovah/Allah's 124,000 automata ever qualified for that divine office. This proves that there is certainly something divine and unique about Jesus Christ of Nazareth.

Indeed, the Bible says that Jesus Christ was something greater than the prophets. He was the Master of the true prophets of the Bible. His expected incarnation into the world was the subject and focus of their prophetic profession. I should reiterate that the linage of the true prophets of the Messiah stopped with John the Baptist, who enjoyed the singular privilege of ushering in the Messiah unto the earthly stage. John the Baptist came to reveal the Messiah to humankind; he did not come with any message from Jehovah/Allah aimed towards reformation of the irredeemable earthly order. It is, in fact, blasphemous to group Jesus Christ, our authoritative heavenly Messiah, amongst the helpless prophets of the world whom Jehovah/Allah simply refers to as his "favored slaves."

Prophet Mohammad of Arabia, for instance, did not even know what would become the final fate of his captive spirit or those of his followers on the last day. He confessed, saying, "I am no new thing among the messengers (of Allah), **nor know I what**

will be done with me or with you. I do but follow that which is inspired in me, and I am but a plain warner. ... "Lo! **I am commanded to worship Allah**, making religion pure for Him (only). And **I am commanded to be the first of those who surrender (unto Him)**. Lo! If I should disobey my Lord, **I fear the doom** of a tremendous Day. Allah I worship, making my religion pure for Him (only)." [Q 46:9; 39:11-14]

In direct contrast, Jesus Christ authoritatively says, "I am the way, and the truth, and the life. ... "I came that they [my followers] may have life, and have it abundantly. I am the Good Shepherd. The good shepherd lays down his life for the sheep." [John 14:6; 10:10-11]

Muhammad was abducted and compelled under duress to become a messenger of Jehovah/Allah. According to the Quran, he was merely one of Allah's numerous *favored slaves*. Jesus Christ is the Master of his divine mission in the world, and he is in absolute harmony with the Father who sent him. He knows where he comes from and where he is taking his redeemed followers to. Muhammad was *commanded* to surrender unconditionally, and to worship Allah, his slave master, and he conceded because he feared fatal reprisal.

It is a documented fact that Muhammad at first refused to be a messenger of Allah but was bullied into submission. He *surrendered* to Allah because he was subdued. Thus, he was a 'forced messenger' of a god who would not even let him know what his ultimate reward or fate would be. Surely, there is no basis upon which anyone can reasonably compare Muhammad and Jesus Christ.

This is what Karen Armstrong narrates in his book, *A History of God*, about how Muhammad became a messenger of Allah:

> "He [Muhammad] said that an angel had appeared to him and given him a curt command: 'Recite!' (iqra!) Like the Hebrew prophets who were often reluctant to utter the

Word of God [Jehovah/Allah], Muhammad refused, protesting 'I am not a reciter!' He was no kahin, one of the ecstatic soothsayers of Arabia who claimed to recite inspired oracles. But, Muhammad said, the angel simply enveloped him in an overpowering embrace, so that he felt as if all the breath was being squeezed from his body. Just as he felt that he could bear it no longer, the angel released him and again commanded him to 'Recite!' (iqra!). Again, Muhammad refused and again the angel embraced him until he felt that he had reached the limits of his endurance. Finally, at the end of a third terrifying embrace, Muhammad found the first words of a new scripture pouring from his mouth."

PARABLE OF THE ROYAL SHIP AND THE BOTTOMLESS DARK OCEAN

To make it easier for people to clearly understand the uniqueness of Jesus Christ with respect to his divine office as the one and only true Messiah of humankind, I need to return to my previous analogy with the ship afloat on the bottomless dark ocean. So many people do not understand why Jesus Christ is the "only Son of the Father in the world," "the only true light that enlightens every man in the world," "the only truth, life and way back to the Father" and "the only guarantor of resurrection and true life" for all fallen dead spirits in the world.

Well, one can liken the Father's heavenly Kingdom to the Royal Ship afloat on the deep dark ocean. The Father is the eternal Captain of the Heavenly Ship, all the ship's crew members are his sons, and they all dwell in absolute bliss onboard as one harmonious household. The entire Royal Ship and its crew are eternally safeguarded by the perfect love and positive influence of the Royal Captain.

Beyond the Royal Ship, the bottomless dark ocean represents the overwhelming Outer Darkness. It is a dangerous, lifeless terrain that is totally devoid of all the familiar essences of perfect existence that characterize life onboard the Royal Ship. The bottomless dark ocean is completely out of bounds for all crew members; none of them can survive or enjoy his natural privileges within the alien satiety.

The eternal principle of safety onboard holds that any crew member that steps beyond his safe bounds on the ship's deck would fall into the bottomless dark ocean and instantly drown. The principle simply states that "Anyone that disregards his natural safe bounds onboard will fall overboard and die." It is common knowledge that is well-entrenched in the subconscious minds of all crew members. And it applies equally to the Royal Captain as it does to even the least crew member onboard the Royal Ship.

This natural standard of safety onboard reechoes the norm of perfect existence in the heavenly Kingdom of the Father, which guarantees eternal life, bliss and safety to every spirit that abides by it. The heavenly norm similarly states that "The spirit that sins shall die." It says in effect, that the only natural place for a living spirit is in the spiritual realm of light and perfection. Beyond this realm is an alien material realm of darkness and lifelessness. Any spirit that strays into this dangerous realm will instantaneously drown spiritually. Any living spirit that strays into this alien realm will automatically forfeit all his perfect spiritual heritages because the realm is totally devoid of all familiar essences of perfect spiritual existence. Allegory of the ship afloat on the bottomless dark ocean goes like this:

Once upon a time, a group of overambitious, self-seeking crew members of the Royal Ship mused over a mystical formula that could enable them to metamorphose into a more pleasurable lifeform within the bottomless dark ocean. They convinced themselves that the magical formula would not only guarantee a carefree existence but would also empower them to completely subdue and transform their new environment, build personal underwater paradises and live as autonomous captains and lords of their own territorial niches.

On one bright sunny day, as many as *one third* of the ship's crew members conspired amongst themselves and chose to take the plunge. As expected, they immediately began to struggle and drown. As the man-overboard alarm signal was sounded, the crews mustered on the main deck and instinctively waited for the Royal Captain's official instructions. Would he become judgmental and order the ship to proceed full ahead on its normal course, or would he overlook the willful misconduct of his drowning crew members and immediately initiate the man-overboard maneuvers to try to rescue them?

Of course, the Royal Captain was not under any obligation to attempt to rescue the rebellious crew members as every crew member was fully entitled to exercise his *free will* and bear the consequences as a free and autonomous individual. The choice to sever their eternal bond with the Royal Ship and its entire crew was absolutely within the inalienable rights of the renegade crew members concerned. They knew the express consequence of their reckless action but felt that they had the perfect solution. So, they were entirely responsible for whatever happened to them within the asphyxiating bottomless dark ocean. If they suffocated to death, they were indeed self-condemned. The Royal Captain owed them nothing and they owed the Royal Ship and its entire crew nothing.

The eternal principle of safety onboard did not contain or imply possible salvation or plan of rescue whatsoever. In any case, no drowning crew member could ever be able to rescue himself or initiate the rescue of anyone else within the death zone. Deciding to initiate the man-overboard maneuvers for their rescue was solely the prerogative of the Royal Captain. But what he would do depended entirely on his personal goodwill and on whether he considered the rescue mission safe for the ship and its law-abiding crew.

Fortunately, the Royal Captain had been a very loving father-figure on his ship. He was, in fact, known and called "the Father" by his entire crew because he extraordinarily loved and cared for the personal needs of both the officers and ratings on his ship. He did not only have the power and means to immediately initiate the man-overboard maneuvers but he whole-heartedly overlooked the willful suicidal action of the fallen crew. Moved by love and extreme compassion, he expectedly willed to rescue them all.

He immediately ordered the special man-overboard maneuvers, also known as the *Williamson's Turn*, and carefully outlined his rescue program to his rescue team, which was headed by his able Chief Officer who was also the official Rescue Officer or Messiah to the drowning crew. The special maneuvers involved turning the ship 180-degrees back on its original track and returning to the exact location where the renegade crews fell overboard. And the aim was to immediately *preserve* the fallen crew from being chopped into pieces by the ship's propeller, as well as make it easier to locate and retrieve them.

The Royal Captain explained that the rescue operation could extend to four phases because of the mystical connotation of the willful suicide. **Firstly**, the Rescue Officer would be lowered into the vicinity of the fall, properly rigged with safety apparatuses and having enough rescue harnesses for the drowning men.

If he still found them in drowning human form, he would attach rescue harness to each in turn and they would be safely hoisted back onboard for necessary medical attention and counseling. They would then resume their normal life activities as human beings onboard. But if they had already activated their mystical formula and metamorphosed into other lifeforms, then the Rescue Officer would have to try to impress his presence on any of the 'new species' who would help him prepare the minds of the others, while he returned onboard to prepare for the second phase.

The **second phase** would involve the Safety Officer returning to the watery deep in whatever form the fallen crew may have assumed. That would be the most dangerous phase of the rescue plan. While in their 'new' form, the Rescue Officer would explain the truth of their past and present situations in their 'new' language so that they will understand him well. He would try his utmost to help them remember that they were happy human beings onboard the Royal Ship, under the command of the most benevolent Captain ever known to humanity. He would prepare their minds for the third phase of the rescue operation.

The **third phase** would involve the ship regularly relaying the Captain's goodwill messages of hope and ultimate salvation direct to their individual minds, through a special radio frequency. It would also involve the use of an interim *re-humanization chamber*, which would be an independent floating rescue raft. Anyone of the fallen crews that willingly renounces the magical formula would be mystical purged or *redeemed* and lifted clear of the death zone. He would be accommodated in the interim re-humanization chamber for necessary first aid and to acclimatize. All redeemed crew members would wait in safety in that chamber till the last willing crew climbed up to safety.

The **final phase** would be the day that the Rescue Officer would safely hoist all the recovered crews within the re-humanization chamber back onboard to be fully restored to their original positions of honor onboard the ship. That would be the day of ultimate merry onboard, on the account of the dead crew that miraculously came back to life. All the remaining fallen crew that willfully rejected the Royal Captain's gracious offer of a *second chance* would have no one else to blame for their perpetual agonies within the bottomless deep ocean but themselves. They would remain self-condemned and gnash their teeth in pain and grief forever.

As can be clearly seen, the Royal Captain's rescue program was a very complex one. The responsibility for its successful implementation within the watery deep rested squarely on the Chief Officer who was the sole Rescue Officer. But the responsibility for the safety of the entire ship, the rescue operation, and possible contingencies rested squarely on the shoulders of the Royal Captain. He would be fully in charge of his command console onboard and would personally oversee the entire emergency. So, the success of the entire rescue operation would depend on absolute harmony of purpose between the Royal Captain and the Rescue Officer.

As the Royal Captain could not possibly abandon his central command position onboard to personally carry out the rescue mission, he needed an envoy who would literally become the physical manifestation of his will within the watery deep. For the practical aspects of the rescue operation to be successful, the Rescue Officer must be genuinely loving, compassionate, and whole-heartedly committed as the Royal Captain. They would literally become one and the same as far as the rescue operation was concerned.

As the rest of the crew members worked in unison towards implementing the Royal Captain's masterplan, the Rescue Officer quickly donned his personal safety diving harnesses as he pledged his absolute allegiance to the Royal Captain. "I know exactly how deeply you feel about this operation, and I am optimistic that it will be successful Captain. I am fully aware of the delicate nature and the dangers involved, and I give you my word of honor that I will willingly pay whatever price it requires to accomplish your will." The Royal Captain nodded his approval and expressed confidence in the Rescue Officer's innate abilities and resolute commitment, and said to him, "Indeed, you and I are one!"

While the ship made delicate maneuvers to keep in sight the exact position of the fall, the crew made the necessary arrangements and lowered the Rescue Officer into the deep dark ocean with enough rescue harnesses for all the drowning crew. But as anticipated, when the Rescue Officer got into the watery deep, there were no drowning men in sight. All he found in the vicinity were some strange fishes, corresponding to the exact number of the fallen crew. He realized therefore, that they had already activated their magical formula and metamorphosed into fishes. How could he then speak to fishes, and hope to convince them that they were really drowning human beings, who urgently needed to be rescued and restored to their *proper* human existence onboard?

He tried to speak to them in human language, but they moped at him with playful excitement and swam around him as if he were a spectacular alien. He told them that the Royal Captain and the entire crew were so worried about them and that they earnestly yearned for their rescue and safe return to the one happy ship where they truly belonged. Unfortunately, they no longer spoke or understood human language. Most of them just flapped their fins vigorously in defiance, made some animal noises, and promptly swam away. Then it dawned on the Rescue Officer that the entire operation would involve the whole four phases as the Royal Captain had projected.

Rescuing drowning human beings, who now looked like, felt like, and believed that they were fishes dwelling in their natural watery environment would surely be a very difficult task. Nevertheless, the Rescue Officer persisted and finally succeeded in conveying the substance of his rescue mission to one intelligent dolphin duo who miraculously understood his human gesturing and signage. He gave them as much information as they could handle considering their present genotype. And he assured them that he would return amongst the dolphins in fish form, so that he would be able to communicate effectively with all the species in their "new" language. He also commissioned the dolphins to disseminate awareness and prepare the minds of the other species about his expected return.

With that accomplished, he signaled the Royal Captain and was hoisted back onboard to deliberate on the next phase of the rescue program. While onboard, the Rescue Officer narrated in detail his findings, actions and great success with the Dolphin Family, and reiterated his solemn determination to see to the successful completion of the entire mission. When the Royal Captain addressed the ship, he stressed his unchanged resolve to retrieve all the fallen crew members that would willingly accept his rescue plan.

Of course, the mystical formula of experimental existence within the watery deep was well-known to every ship crew member but so were the eternal predicaments. The eternal principle of safety onboard did not leave any crew member in any doubt about the immediate and eternal consequences of taking that wrong step into oblivion. It permanently presented every crew member the choice between good and evil, wright and wrong, and life and death.

No right-thinking crew ever bothered to attempt the death plunge because the immediate and eternal consequences were known to be both fatal and overwhelming. While the fleeting death pangs of ordinary human death could be bearable, the agonies of dying endlessly would be insufferable. The asphyxiating dark ocean was not a realm of normal existence but would suffocate all aspects of normal human mentality and natural sense of right and wrong. It was a realm of false living, a region of obsessive meanness, selfishness, greed, opportunism, power mongering, bitter rivalry, ungodliness, conceit, betrayal, rancor, willful oppression and much more.

The overambitious crew neglected the fact that the mystical formula never offered any guaranteed outcome. It never guaranteed that everyone that tried the formula would succeed in becoming *the Lord* or the *Supreme Captain* of the watery deep. Some might become Leviathans, killer whales, killer sharks, sea lions etc., while others might become tuners, salmons, sardines, crayfishes etc. Being a region of utter limitations, opportunism and absolute lawlessness would become the new normal. The strong and mighty would dominate and prey on the weak and helpless, and the winners would happily take it all without feeling any qualms whatsoever.

Life in the deep dark seas would be extremely precarious; it would be strictly a matter of the survival of the fittest. Besides the mighty swallowing up the weak and small, spikes of death were known to litter every nook and cranny of the dangerous satiety and could strike at any moment that one hardly expected it. The smaller fishes were not the only vulnerable ones. Even the bigger fishes that could not be swallowed up by others did not also enjoy peace of mind. Since they depended entirely on killing and eating others to stay alive, the big ones would naturally starve to death too when the smaller fishes became smarter and more difficult to prey upon. Thus, the central essence of the mystical fish life was ultimately self-destruction.

While the Rescue Officer prepared to return for the second phase of his rescue mission, one cunning and scheming Leviathan had already successfully manipulated the existing situation and arrogated to himself false titles as the Supreme Leviathan and Captain of the entire ocean. He had already solidly consolidated his crippling hold on his fellow fallen crew and devised formidable opposition plans to squarely subvert the Rescue Officer's rescue mission when he eventually reappeared in the form of a fish.

The haughty Leviathan had persisted and successfully breached the staunch legacy of the *prophetic* dolphin family through one of their unsuspecting members. He thoroughly brainwashed and conditioned their minds to betray their expected friend and Redeemer when he eventually returns. He had also established strong and effective *religious* propaganda machinery that galvanized all the species. And he recruited a casehardened *porcupine species* as ruthless foot soldiers to terrorize and jeer any slack species into effective opposition. Therefore, the Rescue Officer was not simply going back to preach repentance and redemption to some peaceful, harmless fishes, but rather to battle against the false Captain of the watery deep and against the violent propaganda machinery that he had wittingly set up to thwart the Royal Captain's humanitarian mission.

Evidently, the Supreme Leviathan himself was not in the least interested in personal salvation. His choice of "another life" was premeditated, and he was firmly determined to make rescue as hard as he could for all his beguiled captives. As he considered the complex and seemingly impenetrable nature of his belligerent scheme of opposition against the will of the Royal Captain, he nicknamed himself "God of War." He shook his head and bragged about his radical personal defenses in arrogant defiance to the coming Rescue Officer:

"Can you draw out Leviathan with a fishhook, or press down its tongue with a cord? Can you put a rope in its nose, or pierce its jaw with a hook? Will it make many supplications to you? Will it speak soft words to you? **Will it make a covenant with you to be taken [back onboard] as your servant forever?** Will you play with it as with a bird, or will you put it on leash for your girls? Will traders bargain over it? Will they divide it up among the merchants? Can you fill its skin with harpoons, or its head with fishing spears? **Lay your hands on it, think of the battle; you will not do it again! Any hope of capturing it will be disappointed; were not even the gods overwhelmed at the sight of it? No one is so fierce as to dare to stir it up. Who can stand before it? Who can confront it and be safe?— under [below] the whole heaven who?** ...

Its sneezes flash forth light, and its eyes are like the eyelids of the dawn. From its mouth go flaming torches; sparks of fire leap out. Out of its nostrils comes smoke, as from a boiling pot and burning rushes. Its breath kindles coals, and a flame comes out of its mouth. In its neck abides strength, and terror dances before it. The folds of its flesh cling together; it is firmly cast and immovable. **Its heart is as hard as stone**, as hard as the lower millstone. **When it raises itself up the gods are afraid**; at the crashing they are beside themselves.

Though the sword reaches it, it does not avail, nor does the spear, the dart, or the javelin. It counts iron as straw, and bronze as rotten wood. The arrow cannot make it flee; slingstones, for it, are turned to chaff. Clubs are counted as chaff; it laughs at the rattle of javelins. Its underparts are like sharp potsherds; it spreads itself like a threshing sledge on the mire. **It makes the deep boil like a pot; it makes the sea like a pot of ointment. It leaves a shining wake behind it; one would think the deep to be white-haired. On the earth it has no equal,** *a creature* **without fear. It surveys everything that is lofty;** *it is king over all that are proud.*" [Job 41:1-34 (NRSV)]

The words of the haughty Leviathan reeked of ignorance, pride and arrogance. But real power did not amount to ultra body-armor and vain glory but to successfully setting free the captives of a brutish beast. Nothing would deter the Resue Officer from returning to the watery deep as he promised to accomplish the Royal Captain's will for his fallen crew.

Because the fallen crew had metamorphosed into various species of fishes, the Rescue Officer would likewise reappear as a fish to communicate effectively with them all. He needed to personally convey the truth to them in ways that they would all understand. He would have to help them to remember and contrast their blissful and purposeful life as humans onboard the Royal Ship with their dangerous and aimless existence as fishes in the wild ocean. More especially, he needed to remind them of the fatherly love of the Royal Captain, and to assure them that he still loved and wanted them back to their rightful family. The supreme

Leviathan that now posed as their super *Captain* and best friend, was really their *Captor* and archenemy.

No doubt, the second phase of the Rescue Officer's mission was both difficult and dangerous. It simply represented a clear testament of true love and extreme self-sacrifice for one's friends. The greatest danger involved was not just venturing into an alien and precarious environment as a fish but especially appearing as one of the smallest and most vulnerable species. That way, he would be able to communicate effectively with both the big and, especially, the smaller ones who were the endangered prey. If he appeared as a big fish, the smaller and vulnerable ones would be scared to come around him to hear his good news. But as a small but rare golden fish, he would be able to communicate with both the big and small. He would fearlessly swim around and communicate with the bigger fishes because they would consider him poisonous and therefore, deadly to swallow up.

As expected, the Rescue Officer eventually emerged among the dolphin family as he had promised. But though the older generations of dolphins were his trusted allies, the present generation had forsaken the noble legacies of their family tree. The supreme Leviathan had cunningly infiltrated and brainwashed the family against their expected Messiah. He put them through overwhelming terror and exacted an eternal covenant of total blind allegiance from them. They had become so enthralled to him that they now saw the rare golden fish as their terminal enemy who they must not only chase out of their midst but also kill to save the other species from being eternally contaminated.

He tried to remind them about his friendly encounter with their first parents when he temporarily descended in his natural human form, but none of what he said made sense to them. The supreme Leviathan had cast a strong spell of ignorance over their minds, so, though he now spoke their language they heard, but did not understand him.

Nevertheless, he authoritatively ratified the prophetic words of the true dolphins about him and explained his mission directly to the ones that wished to hear him. He even made more disciples who were ardent and enthusiastic about returning to their normal human existence onboard the Royal Ship. He also established the *re-humanization chamber* as proposed by the Royal Captain, where the rescued fish-humans would undergo full transformation or "rebirth." They would live normal human lives there while waiting in safety for the last willing fallen crew to be set free from the Leviathan's wicked spell of eternal doom.

His mission as a fish was generally a resounding success. It yielded great but gradually unfolding dividends. He was not only able to communicate with the fishes in their own languages but was also able to lead an exemplary lifestyle amongst them that portrayed the glorious nature of human existence onboard. His utterances and actions stuck in their minds and images of the more respectable and creative life onboard gradually began to reverberate in their subconscious minds. His success was not only restricted to the prophetic dolphin family. Many other species were equally rekindled and guided to the re-humanization chamber.

While the Rescue Officer was rounding off the second phase of his mission and preparing to step out of his temporary golden fish cloak, the supreme Leviathan and his accomplices plotted to kill and run him off the watery deep. They calculated that if they could successfully run him off the entire sphere of the deep dark ocean, persecute and kill off all his well-known followers and re-blindfold the borderline enthusiasts, that they would have been able to quash his entire rescue mission. They conspired with some greedy converts from the dolphin family and succeeded as planned. Unknown to them however, the Rescue Officer's disposable fish cloak had already fully served its purpose, and he needed to discard it before resuming his perfect human life onboard.

Before his departure, he had already taught his teaming followers the *human* language and activated the auto radio-wave system approved by the Royal Captain for seamless communication. The Radio-Wave phase was the third phase of the rescue mission. It was intended to steadily beam down the Royal Captain's goodwill messages to the converts, and to explain matters in detail to upgrade their human awareness, even while they were still trapped in the fish world. Anyone that attains adequate enlightenment would be automatically lifted to the re-humanization raft where he must wait until the last savable fallen crew came in.

The third phase was also designated as the protracted *Harvesting Period*, specifically allowed for the gradual and thorough mopping up process, to make sure that not a single savable crew was abandoned in the deep dark ocean. It could also be called the last *Roll Call* or the last *Judgment Phase*. While the willing ones would be rescued and lifted clear of the miserable watery deep, the adamant and unrepentant ones would remain self-condemned to the terrible consequences of their willful choice forever. The Rescue Officer would return at the completion of the radio-wave phase, to perform the final Exodus of all the saved ones in the re-humanization raft or '*interim haven*' from the entire spheres of the watery deep and back onboard as recovered officers and crew with their full status restored.

I am sure that the storyline above clearly captures the human situation in the world. The Royal Ship represents the Father's perfect spiritual Kingdom *above*, while the deep dark ocean *below* stands for the overwhelming Outer Darkness. The patient, loving, and fatherly Royal Captain denotes our ever-loving Father in heaven, while the kind and longsuffering Rescue Officer symbolizes Jesus Christ, the only official Messiah and Rescuer of the fallen dead spirits in the world.

The supreme Leviathan of the bottomless dark ocean is none other than Jehovah/Allah, "who would not let his prisoners go home." [Isaiah 14:17] The mortal fish bodies that the fallen crew adapted for their new watery environment correspond to the mortal organic bodies that fallen dead spirits presently wear in their alien material environment. Viewed in the light of the above analogy, people can now fully understand the uniqueness of Jesus Christ in our world.

KNOWLEDGE IS INEVITABLE FOR SALVATION

Knowledge is power, ignorance breeds irrational trepidation, and fear is death! True spiritual salvation is impossible without knowledge. Therefore, true spiritual salvation is a battle against ignorance and fear of all sorts. Of course, ignorance is not of the Father who is Infinite Knowledge. It is an unnatural state, exploited by oppressors and malevolent minds to suppress and subject their blind victims.

Jehovah/Allah, the god of Eden is the principal exploiter of human ignorance. He willfully denied the humans their divine right to the knowledge of good and evil in the beginning, because he planned to exploit their unnatural state of ignorance forever. He stole knowledge away from them so that he might fool them into believing and looking up to him as God Almighty and as a benevolent being, which he is not. Indeed, only ignorance makes human beings believe that the fallen dead spirit of the mystical man of Eden, is the Living Father Almighty.

To attain spiritual salvation, humans must seek and obtain divine knowledge without fear. They must knowingly confront and confound Jehovah/Allah and all his accomplices who maliciously manipulate human situations to sustain human ignorance. Worldly religion and its operatives stand out as major abettors of the forces that keep humans permanently in the dark. Jehovah/Allah is the principal ruler of the world of ignorant humans and a self-confessed opposer of human enlightenment. Religion serves the evil will of Jehovah/Allah because it is a full-fledged institution of the world.

Jesus Christ is the only true source of human enlightenment. He made that clear during his first advent into the world as Spirit of Knowledge. His eye-opening encounter with Adam and Eve in Eden signaled inauguration of his primary mission of abolishing human ignorance that sustains spiritual captivity of human spirits. Knowledge of good and evil is the basis of comparative reasoning necessary to differentiate *evil* Jehovah/Allah from our *good* heavenly Father and to make sense of the need for urgent spiritual salvation. The heavenly Spirit of Knowledge endowed Adam and Eve with that power of comparative reasoning, and the Scripture says, "then the eyes of both were opened." [Genesis 3:7]

Thereafter, Adam and his descendants prophesied to the whole world that "The true light that enlightens every man was coming into the world." [John 1:9] The last prophet, named John the Baptist, "came as a witness to [finally] testify concerning that light [of knowledge], so that through him all men might believe. [John 1:7]

At its appointed time, the heavenly Spirit of Knowledge incarnated as prophesied in the person of Jesus Christ and ushered in greater enlightenment to the world. And he says, "For this I was born, and for this I have come into the world, to bear witness to the truth. Everyone who is of the truth hears my voice." ... And "If you continue in my word, you are truly my disciples, and you will *know* the truth, and the truth will make you free." [John 18:37; 8:31-32]

The battle against ignorance and spiritual captivity involves acquiring knowledge of certain truths that show clearly that Jehovah/Allah is the Evil One. Spiritual salvation is impossible for anyone who does not discover these truths. But these truths are *forbidden* by Jehovah/Allah, and human religion cannot reveal them to anyone because it is of the world. In fact, the world is terminally opposed to people who genuinely seek knowledge and the truths that Jesus Christ ministers to the world. *The Final Testaments* treatise informs, encourages, and gives true sense of direction to genuine seekers of spiritual salvation.

True spiritual salvation is a battle for people who are honest and courageous. According to the Scripture, it is not a battle against fellow human beings but "*against the principalities, the powers, the world rulers of this present darkness, and the spiritual hosts of wickedness in the heavenly places.*" Sadly, not many people know exactly who *the principalities and world rulers of this present darkness* are.

They include Jehovah/Allah, the faceless archangels, and all their human viceroys that superintend over the three symbiotic arms of the oppressive worldly government—secular, religious and underworld. These together, form the inglorious "*powers that be*" of the world. Jehovah/Allah stands at the apex of the inglorious "*powers that be*" and he is the principal idol of all human religions.

While the **secular** rulers of the world deliberately create socioeconomic anguish for the helpless masses with their oppressive policies, **religious** rulers lure the desperate masses into eternal spiritual captivity, and the lawless operatives of organized **underworld** attack and undermine the moral fabrics of true humanity. These operatives are directly and indirectly in league with the *heavenly banditti* that the Scripture refers to as *spiritual hosts of wickedness in the heavenly places*. Genuine seekers of true spiritual salvation can only confront and overcome the ruthless "*powers that be*" with the help of Jesus Christ.

That "the fear of Jehovah is the beginning of wisdom," is a very cheap Old Testament religious propaganda. No truly enlightened mind buys that lie anymore. The Jewish experience has proved decisively that the fear of Jehovah can only lead to primitivism, religious hypocrisy and extremism. Jehovah/Allah is a toothless Lion of Judah. Being afraid of him can only lead one to eternal spiritual death. The Scripture says that we should rather resist him "and he will flee from us." [James 4:7]

The truth is that the Father is Love, and those who love him have nothing whatsoever to fear in the world. As the Scripture says, "There is no fear in love, but perfect love casts out fear. ... and he who fears is not perfected in [the] love [of the Father and of his Christ]." [1 John 4:18] Hence, *The Final Testaments* calls on those who fight the good fight of eternal spiritual salvation in the name of Jesus Christ to do so without fear of the twice beaten Jehovah/Allah. People who fight with knowledge of truth will discover that winning the battle becomes a satisfying formality.

Finally, to "choose" to live, one must knowingly "refuse" to die. But to know the difference, one must endeavor to be fully informed. To know the whole truth is the inalienable divine right of every fallen spirit in the world. Neither Jehovah/Allah nor any of his minions have the right to usurp that. So, Jesus Christ says that we should "have no fear of them; for nothing is covered that will not be revealed, or hidden [by Jehovah/Allah] that will not be know." [Matthew 10:26]

JESUS CHRIST AND THE FATHER ARE ONE; JEHOVAH/ALLAH IS ONE WITH THE WORLD

I stated categorically in a previous volume that Jehovah does not share the same qualities with Jesus Christ. This simple statement of fact is supported by overwhelming historical and scriptural evidence. It holds serious implications for people who erroneously believe that Jehovah is the father of Jesus Christ.

Most religious believers, Jews and customary Christians, feel outraged by any truth that suggests that Jehovah is indeed Antichrist. Rather than objectively looking at the mental and spiritual challenges raised by that truth, many of them threaten '*fire of holy ghost*' in the name of Jehovah against anyone who dares to highlight such distinction. They tow the path of religious fanaticism rather than the path of reason and common sense.

Once, when I appeared on a call-in TV show called "Issues and Answers" to speak on *The Final Testaments* to Nigerian audience, one fanatic lover of Jehovah assailed me at the waiting room of the TV Station. He heaped all sorts of bitter insults and curses on me and called me all sorts of derogatory names. And finally, clinching his fists and teeth, he said to me, "I feel like strangling you right now." But I calmly asked him, "In the name of which "God" do you feel like strangling me now; in the name of Jesus Christ, the Prince of Peace or in the name of Jehovah, the unforgiving god of violence and wars?" At hearing that, he quickly dropped his clinched fist and faked a friendly outlook. "I mean that you must ask *God* to forgive you, and I know that he will if you repent," he concluded.

But as we all know, "a vulture does not beget a dove." Jesus Christ himself says that "no good tree bears bad fruit, nor again does a bad tree bear good fruit; for each tree is known by its own fruit. For figs are not gathered from thorns, nor are grapes picked from a bramble bush." [Luke 6:43-44] He says clearly that he and his own Father share the same perfect attributes of loving-kindness. "**I and the Father are one**," he says. ... "He who has seen me has seen the Father, ... "If you had known me, you would have known my Father also; henceforth you know him and have seen him [in me]." [John 10:30; 14:9, 7]

Surely, no honest human being will pretend to see Jehovah in any of the things that Jesus Christ said and did when he was here on earth. Their desires and modus operandi were rather diametrically opposed.

The greatest irony of human religion is that it preaches the goodness of the Father who truly loves and cares for helpless humans but worships and upholds the devilish desires of Jehovah who holds humankind captive on earth. Thus, the world is full of blind religious believers who love and adore the Father deep in their spirits, but do not know him at all. Although Jehovah remains the undisputed god of the world, he is certainly not the Father of Jesus Christ, who transcends the entire material universe.

Jehovah is not the Father, and he is not one with Jesus Christ. While the entire humankind has known, interacted with, and worshipped Jehovah since Eden, only very few people have been privileged to discover the Father and his true Christ. Hence, Jesus Christ says that "no one knows the Son except the Father, and **no one knows the Father except the Son and any one to whom the Son chooses to reveal him.**" [Matthew 11:27]

It is important therefore, that genuine seekers of true spiritual salvation must make effort to distinguish the Father from Jehovah, god of Eden. It is important that one does not mistake deadly hemlock for the invigorating parsley. Right-thinking people do not drink seawater just because it is widely available; they search diligently for life-giving fresh water. Genuine seekers of spiritual salvation should seek diligently for *the truly living spring*. Jesus Christ is the Living Spring, and he says, "Everyone who drinks of this [worldly] water will thirst again, but whoever drinks of the water that I shall give him will never thirst; the water that I shall give him will become in him a spring of water **welling up to eternal life**." [John 4:13-14]

Because Jesus Christ is one with the Father who is the Tree of Eternal Life, he is the only way that leads to spiritual restoration and eternal life for all fallen dead spirits in the world. Indeed, he says, "I am the resurrection and the life. Anyone who believes in me will live, even after dying." And "I am the way, the truth, and the life. No one can come to the Father except through me." [John 11:25; 14:6(NLT)]

So, while Jesus Christ holds the key to true life eternal, Jehovah "hold the keys of death and Hades." [Revelation 1:18NLT)] Jehovah is a deadly hemlock; people who mistake him for the loving Father of Jesus Christ are bound to share in his impending eternal doom. The gospel is simple and clear on that.

I also made it emphatic in a previous volume that Jehovah is the Chief Devil and self-arrogated God of the lost world of ignorant humans. He is everything that describes the Devil. He is arrogant, self-conceited, greedy, self-seeking, jealous, violent, oppressive, wrathful, unforgiving and expressly committed to leading captive human spirits to the "*second*" eternal spiritual death. Moreover, he is openly opposed to everything that Jesus Christ, our Messiah, exemplifies. He is the Antichrist, and the principal obstacle to human salvation. And remarkably, both the Bible and the Islamic Quran that are largely inspired by him testify to these facts. No amount of religious baloney will be able to erase Jehovah/Allah's self-incriminating utterances and deeds that are captured on the pages of these scriptures, as well as documented in human history.

In contrast, Jesus Christ is a tried-and-tested humanitarian. He is gentle, peaceable, kind, loving, forgiving, and more. He possessed and exemplified every attribute expected of the true envoy of our loving heavenly Father. His utterances and deeds proved beyond every reasonable doubt that he was genuinely committed toward the spiritual salvation of captive human spirits trapped in the world. Not even his sworn enemies could fault his impeccable personality. He is supremely qualified as the true Messiah of captive human spirits.

Jesus Christ differs from Jehovah/Allah in so many crucial ways. He is the "Prince of Peace," while Jehovah is the "prince of war" and author of violence. Jesus Christ came into the world to rekindle fallen dead spirits and lead them back to the Father who is the divine Tree of eternal life. Jehovah/Allah forbids spiritual enlightenment for captive human spirits and sets obstacles on their way back to the Father. The Genesis account of the battle of Eden captures the clear divergence between the oppressive will of Jehovah/Allah, god of Eden, and the redemptive will of the heavenly Christ.

Jesus Christ loves, prays and works for the good, even, of those who hate and plot against his divine mission in the world, but Jehovah/Allah expressly hates those who do not serve his devilish interests. Jesus Christ came into the world to give life to fallen dead spirits. Hence he says, "I came that they may have life, and have it abundantly. ..." "For this is the will of my Father, that everyone who sees the Son and believes in him **should have eternal life**; and **I will raise him up at the last day**." [John 10:10; 6:40]

Jehovah/Allah, on the other hand, vowed to avenge his humiliating defeat in Eden against defenseless humans and to lead as many fallen human spirits as possible to eternal spiritual death. He never talks about giving life to anyone, or about helping human beings to reach the Father who is the Divine Tree that gives eternal life. His "Last Judgment" only talks about "blood and fire and columns of smoke," about the killing field of "Armageddon," and how he would ultimately slaughter and destroy entire humanity.

His sole aim in this life is to dominate and hold human spirits captive forever. Accordingly, he says:

- "Jehovah is a jealous God and avenging; Jehovah is avenging and wrathful; Jehovah takes vengeance on his adversaries and keeps wrath for his enemies." [Nahum 1:2]

- "Jehovah is enraged against all the nations, and furious against all their host, he has doomed them, has **given them over for slaughter**." [Isaiah 34:2]

- "Therefore, wait for me," says Jehovah, "**for the day** when I arise as a witness. For my decision is to gather nations, to assemble kingdoms, to pour out upon them my indignation, all the heat of my anger; for in the fire of my jealous wrath **all the earth shall be consumed**." [Zephaniah 3:8]

- "I will not be sad about the large number of people [fallen human spirits] who will be lost [at the last day], because even now they last no longer than a vapor; they disappear like fire and smoke; they catch fire, blaze up, and quickly go out." [2 Esdras 7:61(GNB)]

- And "I will fill hell with the jinn and mankind together." [Quran 32:13]

Since the days of Eden, Jehovah/Allah's devilish desires have consistently contradicted the divine will of our loving heavenly Father and hence that of Jesus Christ, our Messiah. The will of the Father has always been that his fallen dead sons in the Outer Darkness might regain their lost spiritual nature. It has never been his will that any of us should remain dead and lost in the world but that we might regain eternal life as his beloved sons of resurrection.

The Redeeming Spirit of Knowledge conveyed the Father's gracious will to Adam and Eve in Eden for the first time. Unsurprisingly, Jehovah/Allah god of Eden branded him serpent and evil, but he authoritatively promised that Adam and his posterity "will not surely die" as god of Eden had threatened.

At the appointed time, the Redeeming Spirit of Knowledge incarnated among Adam's posterity as Jesus Christ and reaffirmed his promise to grant eternal life to every fallen dead spirit in the world that accepts his divine word of life. "I am the resurrection and the life. Anyone who believes in me will live, even after dying," he assures. [John 11:25(NLT)] He also affirmed the Father's will in human language to all and sundry, saying, "So, it is not the will of my Father who is in heaven that one of these little ones should perish." [Matthew 18:14]

Jehovah/Allah god of Eden tried once again to dismiss him as, yet another "serpent" and "sinner," but enlightened humanity would no longer buy the blatant lie from him. People are better informed now and therefore, have no doubt that Jesus Christ is indeed the only hope of spiritual resurrection for all the fallen dead spirits in the world.

Adam and Eve lived in total ignorance in Eden and were completely beguiled by the brazen lies that the God of Eden told them. He told them that knowing the difference between what is good and what is evil would cause them to die. He, therefore, forbade them ever to seek to know. He freely posed as *God Almighty* to them, while denying them knowledge of their truly loving heavenly Father and their divine heritage in him.

Without the knowledge of good and evil, Adam and Eve had no way of knowing that God of Eden was evil, and the Father was good. That way, he also prevented them from taking advantage of the Father's gracious offer of spiritual rebirth. Of course, one must first know that a better life exists somewhere before he will genuinely desire a rebirth.

So, Jehovah/Allah, the god of Eden, is the principal obstacle in the way of humans' spiritual salvation. He vehemently disapproved of humans' right to spiritual enlightenment from the onset and thus, knowingly opposes the Father's divine will. In contrast, the heavenly Spirit of Knowledge promised that knowledge will not lead humans to death. He later incarnated as Jesus Christ and reaffirms that knowledge rather leads to spiritual freedom and eternal life. He affirms that knowledge will help us to know the truth, and that only the truth will set us free. Then he reiterated his promise, saying that those who believe in him will surely live, even after dying. "Truly, truly, I say to you, if anyone keeps my word, **he will never see death**," he assures. [John 8:51]

The Quran affirms that Jesus Christ is the Messiah and that he is indeed of the Righteous Father, while the Bible confirms that he is the Good Shepherd that leads all willing dead spirits back to the

Father who is the Tree of Life. Jesus Christ authoritatively says to the world, "I am the way, and the truth, and the life; no one comes to the Father, but by me." [John 14:6] But Jehovah/Allah personally places both physical and mystical obstacles in the way. Genesis 3:24 (GNB) reads: "Then at the east side of the garden he [Jehovah] put living creatures and a flaming sword which turned in all directions [representing positive obstacles in the way]. [And] **This was to keep anyone from coming near the tree that gives life.**"

Jehovah/Allah's actions and utterances speak his mind clearly. Barricading the way to the Father was a clear act of opposition to the divine mission of Jesus Christ in the world.

Although he tries to impersonate both Jesus Christ and the Father, he never pretends to be in any position to offer true eternal life to any of his devotees. All that he has ever promised humankind in the world is doom and eternal destruction. "I will take vengeance, and **I will spare no man**," remains his prominent mantra. [Isaiah 47:3] These make him the Antichrist and archenemy of true humanity.

These facts are clearly documented in the various worldly scriptures. Yet many religious believers pretend not to see the difference between Jesus Christ and Jehovah/Allah, god of the world. Some readers wanted to know which 'Jehovah' I refer to in my books. "Is Jehovah not the same as Jehovah Sabaoth, 'the Lord of Hosts,' someone once asked me, "how then can you say that the Almighty God that the entire humankind has worshiped since the beginning of the world is the Devil?"

Some said to me, "It looks as if you are saying that Jehovah is not the Father of Jesus Christ." Others accused me of not believing in the Holy Bible. "By the way, which Church do you attend or where do you worship?" some mockingly asked me. Even my younger brother had a question for me. "I have asked you this question before, but let me ask it again," he said. "If the Father's love for us is as wonderful as you claim, why then has he abandoned us in this world to be dominated and endlessly tormented by Jehovah, whom you call the Devil?"

Many pastors and proponents of religious traditions angrily questioned my ordination or calling that qualified me to dabble into spiritual matters that are far beyond me. They expected me to possess a university degree in Theology or Philosophy of Religion to be ratified by them. Some of them vehemently picked offence with my choice of *"The Final Testaments"* as the title of my works. "How can you speak of your mere 'personal convictions' as the "Final" in the Gospel of Jesus Christ when you are not even an ordained minister of the Word," they asked.

Well, to answer the first part of their question I simply read out my statement of authority as contained in the introduction to volume one of *The Final Testaments*: It reads: *"**My only authority is Jesus Christ of Nazareth**, who alone created the real basis for the genuine application of reason to the issue of "God" and human salvation."* True inspiration from Jesus Christ cannot be learnt from worldly institutions of knowledge. People who consider themselves authorities in religious matters should acknowledge that fact. It would also be in their own interest to appreciate that they can indeed gain deeper insight about spiritual salvation by Jesus Christ from people who are not "ordained" by the Church or the schools.

To the second part of their question, I made it known to them that I did not really "choose" the title that I thought would be popular with editors, publishers, and book buyers, or one that religious authorities of the world would approve of. It came to me, and I could not alter it even if I had tried. *The Final Testaments* represents the unique corpus of end-time testimonies to the divine mission of Jesus Christ. He personally alluded to it as 'the gospel of the Kingdom' in Matthew 24:14 where he says, "And this gospel of the Kingdom will be preached throughout the whole world, as a testimony to all nations; and then the end will come."

My works are not the first of this divine collection and they will certainly not be the last. What I can assure the world is that in the next 200 to 300 years, *The Final Testaments* would have become the truer Bible for all true Christ-followers on the earth. The testamentary New Testament books of John can easily be called the first in the line of *The Final Testaments*. The books plainly testify the difference between our truly loving heavenly Father and Jehovah/Allah, the god of our present world of darkness. John's books were also the first to explain the true personality of Jesus Christ in plain words.

John captures the true nature of Jesus Christ, as the miraculous incarnation of the Father's Will on earth. He was the physical expression of the Divine Word of Life that the Father spoke in heaven for our fallen dead spirits in the world. John 3:16 is the whole gospel of Jesus Christ presented in a very small sentence— **"For the Father so loved the world that he gave his *only* Son, that whoever believes in him should not perish but have eternal life."**

When we add John 1:1, 14, 18 to that, we have all that we need to know about the true spiritual status of Jesus Christ as the Divine Incarnation of the Father's Will in the world.

They read: "In the beginning was the Word, and the Word was with the Father, and the Word was the Father. ... "And the Word became flesh and dwelt among us, full of grace and truth; we have beheld his glory, glory as of the *only* Son from the Father. ... "No one has seen the Father; the *only* Son, who is in the bosom of the Father, he has made him known [in the world]."

Jesus Christ did not only make the Father known in the world, but he also gives all his true disciples the right to become children of the Father. "But to all who believed him and accepted him, **he gave the right to become children of the Father**" says John 1:12-13(NLT). "They are reborn—not with a physical birth resulting from human passion or plan, but a birth that comes from the Father." So, I find the concerns of people who argue that I am not an 'ordained authority' in religious matters entirely irrelevant. Besides, if I were ordained by a religious sect, I would have been expert only at interpreting the will of that sect and not the will of the Father that Jesus Christ inspires. And that is the only thing that matters.

The most important thing is that whatever I have written about Jesus Christ and the Father remains nothing but the truth about them forever. I have heard many religious apologists argue that what Jehovah/Allah inspired his prophets to do and say of him in the Old Testament were only appropriate for the level of peoples' spiritual enlightenment at the time. They argue that Jehovah/Allah had to change or update his messaging with the coming of Jesus Christ into the world.

Indeed, the light of Jesus Christ forced Jehovah/Allah deeper into darkness and he stopped fomenting nuisance openly within human communities. He had to depend entirely on the use of radical human proxies. But everything that his prophets said about him in the Old Testaments remains as true today as they were in the past. Jehovah is still "a man of war," he is still "a jealous god," "he kills and makes alive; he wounds and heals," and he still "brings material blessings and causes human disasters."

Jehovah/Allah's detailed instructions on ritualistic worship, religious intolerance, and blood sacrifices, including animal and human sacrifices are still adhered to by his devotees howbeit, disguised in plain sight. Yet his disciples argue that he upgraded his murderous lifestyle with the coming of Jesus Christ. Such argument merely sounds like one attempting to fetch water with a basket. And it does not speak well of someone who expects enlightened humans to accept that he has suddenly abandoned all his evil ways, transformed into a "King of Peace," and became the true Father of Jesus Christ who is the Prince of Peace.

If a God inspired prophets to say something about him that could not stand the test of time; if the things they say about him could be altered, invalidated or improved upon in later days, then such a God is a gambler. Most certainly, he was not the eternal Father of Lights "with whom there is no variation or shadow due to change." Since Jehovah/Allah inspired his trusted messengers in the past to proclaim him as the "god of war," as "a jealous, wrathful and vengeful god," and as the "god who kills and brings calamity upon humankind," their testimonies should stand forever, otherwise he is simply an impostor.

The perfect attributes of Jesus Christ and our true heavenly Father stand forever. Whatever I say about them in *The Final Testaments* and in my other write-ups should stand the test of time. Therefore, only the future will declare whether I had been divinely destined as one of the humble contributors to the divinely ordained corpus or not.

However, I was not overly surprised or deterred by opinions of people who considered me unqualified to talk on issues about 'God.' I knew that the contempt and reproach could be worse. It was obvious to me, however, that the people who never even bothered to read the books were the ones that readily jumped to conclusions. If they did, they would have discovered the liberating truth. But as the Scripture says, 'people perish for lack of knowledge.'

Indeed, people's reaction to novel ideas that challenge religious traditions, such as the ones expressed in *The Final Testaments*, is always spontaneous and uncompromising. They would simply jump to some fail-safe religious conclusions before they have had time to even read and understand the issues raised. In fact, customary religions of the world deliberately discourage their laity from reading and scrutinizing even their own religious beliefs. Jehovah/Allah personally empowers all kinds of religious charlatans, popes, bishops, priests, pastors, imams, gurus, etc. to steal away peoples' rights to direct intuitive information.

Somehow, it has become universally accepted that only this group of religious 'slaves of Jehovah/Allah' have the right to read, understand, and explain the Scriptures to the rest of humanity. But some of these so-called religious authorities are borderline illiterates. Most of them are largely ignorant and suffer from spiritual poverty. Yet well-educated and better-informed individuals, willingly allow themselves to be subjected under their spell of ignorance.

It is only in the names of religion and Jehovah/Allah that some blind teachers who think that they see teach people who see but refuse to acknowledge what they see. Allowing such charlatans to read and interpret the *books* to them, which they are really in a better position to read and understand themselves, means religious believers knowingly surrendering the eternal fate of their precious spirits in the hands of their archenemies. Truly enlightened people will never allow themselves to be boxed into some religious cocoons.

Edenic humans were knowledgeless; they were spiritually blind. Their sudden encounter with the heavenly Spirit of Knowledge marked the beginning of mankind's evolution in knowledge. But religious 'slaves of Jehovah/Allah' branded the redeeming heavenly Teacher a serpent. He must have been a unique type of "Serpent" indeed. First, he opened the spiritual eyes of Edenic humans and literally sent them to school. And we have all benefited from the very school that the heavenly Spirit of Knowledge inaugurated in Eden for Adam and Eve and their teaming posterity. Humanity acquired the knowledge of good and evil against the will of Jehovah/Allah and has since learnt a lot from the school of this life.

Next, the heavenly Spirit of Knowledge incarnated amongst us in the person of Jesus Christ of Nazareth to enable us to apply our acquired mental abilities to figure out all the truths about our present situation. He further activated subconscious minds in his true disciples and empowered them with the Holy Spirit of Truth to inwardly inform and guide them through their individual quests toward full spiritual self-realization. So, every true disciple of Jesus Christ is sufficiently schooled in the love of the Father and does not need the eternal yoke of bondage that religious guidance of Jehovah/Allah's votaries represents.

Sadly, most religious believers have not yet realized that it is up to every individual human being to try to know all that is necessary for the salvation of his own spirit. They usually argue that they are too occupied in their own professions to have time to encroach into other people's professions. "It is the profession of religious teachers to read and interpret the scriptures to people of other professions, so we must listen to them," they say. This is the stereotypical attitude of traditional religious believers in general, and it is very unfortunate. Humans are naturally shortsighted. They do not have time for issues of distant spiritual glory, but they willingly work overtime for the material glories of the here and now.

Humans are equally under Jehovah/Allah's terminal spell of ignorance and inaction. It will take time and the special grace of the Father to alter people's indifference toward matters of their own personal spiritual salvation. *The Final Testaments* books are ordained for this crucial time and phase of Christ's redemptive mission for the spiritual salvation of captive human spirits. While it is beyond my power to adequately disseminate the Good News of the Kingdom as fast and effectively as I would love to, *The Final Testaments* would still be preached "throughout the whole world, as a testimony to all nations" as the Messiah foretold.

Now is the appointed time to begin the final testimonies of Christ's gospel of the Kingdom without the habitual fear of Jehovah/Allah. The central truth remains unchanged. It is the express will of the Father to give us eternal life. But is it our will to receive it from Jesus Christ, our only Messiah? Only Jesus Christ can open people's inner eyes and dispel Jehovah/Allah's spell of ignorance over them. Only he can redeem humanity from eternal bondage to Jehovah/Allah, the son of perdition.

Although Jehovah/Allah has been in the business of opposition to the divine mission of Jesus Christ since his shameful defeat in Eden, he remains a loser to this day. People who courageously embrace the truth even today will most certainly overcome him. He may have been the only "God" ever known to human beings since the beginning of this world, but it would eventually become obvious to all and sundry that he has been nothing but an impostor. This "gospel of the Kingdom" will soon force him to show his real self openly.

Honest seekers of spiritual salvation should read and consider the crucial points raised in *The Final Testaments*, as the Holy Spirit of truth directs them. The Father prepared humans for this very crucial point in time by first sending the heavenly Christ into Eden as Spirit of Knowledge to endow us with knowledge of good and evil, functional minds and the good conscience. When we read all scriptures and the gospel of Jesus Christ objectively, we will understand because we already carry the good conscience, and the Holy Spirit of the Father dwells in us. The truth is one, so everyone who is of the truth will hear the silent voice of our Good Shepherd in the pages of the Old Testament, the New Testaments, and *The Final Testaments*.

JESUS CHRIST AS THE ONLY SON OF THE FATHER IN THE WORLD

It is extremely remarkable that the following assertions apply only to Jesus Christ of Nazareth, and not to any other god, prophet or entity in this world. He is *"the only Son of the living Father," "the only true Messiah," "the only true Light that enlightens every man," "the only Way back to the Father"* and *"the only Resurrection and Life"* for any repentant fallen dead spirit in the world. Such unique set of divine authentications ought not to be taken for granted by any right-thinking human being. Sadly, multitudes of religious believers, as well as religious operatives who think of themselves as ordained religious authorities of the world willfully refuse to acknowledge the obvious truth. Jesus Christ is simply unlike any entity ever known and worshiped by humans on planet Earth.

With such outstanding divine credentials, one wonders why even some people who call themselves Christians cannot still distinguish Jesus Christ and his truly loving Father from the bungling, wrathful, and murderous Jehovah/Allah who is clearly an impostor. The consistent desire of the Father and Jesus Christ to give light and life to captive human spirits directly contrast that of Jehovah/Allah who holds the keys, not of light and eternal life, but of Death and Hades.

Jehovah/Allah is cryptically denoted as "the Tree of Zaqqum" in the Quran. The tree of Zaqqum is also "the tree of Death and Hades," and it symbolically stands at the center of our hellish world. Jehovah/Allah is that tree of Zaqqum, as he himself says, "I am the first and the last, ... and I have the keys of Death and Hades." [Revelation 1:17-18] The Quran says, "Lo! the tree of Zaqqum, [is] the food of the sinner! ... Lo! **it is a tree that springeth in the heart of hell. Its crop [fruits] is as it were the heads of devils**." [Quran 44:43-44; 37:64-65] Then it goes further to say, "Unto Allah belongeth whatsoever is in the heavens and whatever is in the earth; and unto Allah all things are returned. ... "Unto him is the return of all of you; it is a promise of Allah in truth." [Quran 3:109; 10:4] In other words, Jehovah/Allah, the tree of Zaqqum, is the cryptic womb of the world to which transmigrating fallen dead spirits return.

The Quran also refers to Jehovah/Allah as "the Consuming One," and says that people who do not believe in the tree of Zaqqum, "every slandering traducer," and wealthy people "who think that their wealth would render them immortal" will be flung to it in the end. Quran 104:4-7 says, "Nay, but verily he [they] will be flung to **the Consuming One**. Ah, what will convey unto thee what the Consuming One is! **(It is) the fire of Allah**, kindled, which leapeth up over the hearts (of men)." So, the difference is really very clear.

By tracing the human genealogy of Jesus Christ among the sons of Adam, the Bible seeks and sells the erroneous impression that Jesus Christ is simply one of the fallen dead spirits that the Father graciously reserves in the Outer Darkness for a second chance. If the Bible is right, then Jesus Christ cannot be "the only Son that the Father sent into the world" from his perfect heavenly Kingdom to redeem the fallen dead spirits in it. If he is one of us, he will be as helpless as we are and therefore will not be able to save any of us. But John 3:16 says that "the Father **sent his only Son** that whoever believes in him should not perish but have eternal life."

The above statement makes it explicit that **the Father's only Son** dwelt in absolute harmony with the Father in his heavenly domain before he commissioned and **"sent"** him into the nether world to rescue his fallen dead sons trapped there. As we saw from the Royal Ship analogy, the Royal Captain **"sent"** the Chief Officer as the *only* Rescue Officer into the watery deep to rescue the drowning crew.

Surely, the Chief Officer was not one of the drowning crew in the watery deep. If he were, the Royal Captain would not be able to send him, and he would not be able to rescue even himself or any of his drowning colleagues. Also, the Chief Officer was not the only upright officer left onboard with the Royal Captain after the fall. But he was certainly the most eligible and the *only* Envoy that the Royal Captain authorized and "sent" for the complex rescue mission.

The Chief Officer wholeheartedly shared the Royal Captain's resolute will about rescuing the drowning crew. He enjoyed direct communication with the Royal Captain on all aspects of the complex rescue mission. Furthermore, the Chief Officer had the unique privilege of descending to the watery deep and ascending back onboard the Royal Ship as required by the rescue plan. No other crew, whether onboard or within the watery deep was as empowered as the Chief Officer regarding the rescue mission. He was simply unique in his office as the *sole* Rescue Officer from the Royal Captain. Every drowning crew would need to undergo the process of *rebirth* in the re-humanization chamber before he could set his feet back onboard the Royal Ship, and that could only take place on the very **last day** of the entire protracted rescue mission.

This is precisely what the Scripture tries to explain in the book of John where it says, "No one [in this world] has ever seen the Father [after the spiritual fall]; the only Son, who is in the bosom of the Father, he has made him known." [John 1:18] Jesus Christ personally says, "Truly, truly, I say to you, unless one is born anew, he cannot see the Kingdom of the Father." By this, he reaffirms the fact that it is impossible for any fallen dead spirit in the world to "ascend and descend" into and from the Father's perfect glorious Kingdom before the official Day of Resurrection.

Jesus Christ made it explicit that even the redeemed spirits that are already in the Interim Paradise cannot proceed to the Father's heavenly Kingdom until the last day of the final phase of the Father's salvation program, when he, as the *sole* Rescue Officer, would officially present them before the Father in his Kingdom. Accordingly, he says in John 6:40, "For this is the will of my Father, that everyone who sees the Son and believes in him should have eternal life; **and I will raise him up [only] at the last day**."

If Jesus Christ is one of the fallen dead spirits in this world, he will not be our sole redeemer, and he will not enjoy the unique privilege of descending and ascending from and to the heavenly Kingdom of the Father until he has undergone the full process of spiritual rebirth himself.

The so-called Old Testament of the Bible gives the erroneous impression that Jehovah/Allah dwells in heaven and that his messengers or *favored slaves* readily ascend to heaven at completion of their earthly assignments. Genesis 5:24 says that "Enoch walked with [Jehovah] *God*; and he was not, for [Jehovah]

God took him [to heaven]." Also, 2 King 2:1, 11 says, "Now when [Jehovah] *God* was about to take Elijah up to heaven by a whirlwind, Elijah and Elisha were on their way from Gilgal. ... And as they still went on and talked, behold, a chariot of fire and horses of fire separated the two of them. And Elijah went up by a whirlwind into heaven."

These were merely narrow-minded mystical stunts stage-managed by Jehovah/Allah. They only exposed him as an impostor, dwelling in false heaven. We know for certain now that neither Enoch nor Elijah went anywhere beyond the earth's atmosphere.

Speaking in his official capacity as the *only* Son of the Father in the world, Jesus Christ authoritatively debunked all Jehovah/Allah's mystical-ascent stunts as false insinuations. He rather stated that "No one [not Jehovah/Allah, or any of his so-called archangelic partners; not Enoch or Elijah or any other prophet for that matter] has ascended into [the Father's glorious] heaven but he who descended from heaven [and became] the Son of man [for the purpose of his redemptive mission]." [John 3:13]

Jesus Christ went further to stress that even with all the melodramatic fanfare with the chariots and horses of fire and whirlwind, Elijah's true position did not even equal the status of the least upright member of the true Kingdom of Heaven. Concerning Elijah, he said, "Truly, I say to you, among those born of women there has arisen no one greater than John the Baptist; **yet he who is least in the Kingdom of heaven is greater than he**. ... and if you are willing to accept it, he [John the Baptist] is Elijah who is to come. He who has ears to hear, let him hear." [Matthew 11:11, 14-15]

Besides, "No one [in the world] knows the Son except the Father, and no one knows the Father except the Son and any one to whom the Son chooses to reveal him," he says. [Matthew 11:27] Even though the Holy Spirit of truth is presently illuminating peoples' minds about the Father and rekindling their dormant spirits, no fallen spirit in the world has seen or will ever see the Father before the last day of Christ's salvation program. None can even peep into the Father's spiritual Heaven before the final Day of Resurrection. On that day, the heavenly Christ would return in his true divine nature, glory and authority as the Father's only true Rescue Officer to perform the actual resurrection of all redeemed spirits, which would include all the ones that ever made it to the Interim Paradise.

Hence, Jesus Christ reaffirms, "Do not murmur among yourselves. No one can come to me unless the Father who sent me draws him; **and I will raise him up [only] at the last day**. It is written in the prophets, 'And they shall all be taught by [the Holy Spirit of] the Father.' Everyone who has heard and learned from the Father comes to me. **Not that anyone has seen the Father except him who is from the Father; he [alone] has seen the Father**." [John 6:43-47]

Remarkably, Jesus Christ says to all his disciples at the close of his earthly ministry, "I am ascending to *my* Father and *your* Father, to *my* God and *your* God." [John 20:17] He calls us sons of the Father because, so we are, yet he is in a unique way, the *only* Son of the Father in the world. While we are fallen *dead* sons of the Father, Jesus Christ is the only *living* Son of the Father in the world. Hence, he remained in absolute harmony with the Father even in the Outer Darkness, which was why he could rightly say, "I and the Father are one." [John 10:30]

If Jesus Christ is fallen and dead as we are, he will not have the authority to forgive our original sin. He will not be able to rescue us from the consequences of our spiritual indiscretions. But we all "beheld his glory, glory as of the only Son from the Father." [John 1:14] Today, we can all bear witness that the heavenly Christ is a *living* Spirit and therefore, one with the Father indeed. He is both a free Spirit and in perfect harmony with the Supreme Father of all Origins whose will he has come into the world to actualize among us. Only a free citizen can bail out his own brothers held in prison custody. "So, if the Son makes you free, you will be free indeed," says John 8:36.

As we saw in the Royal Ship analogy, all the fishes in the deep dark ocean had their origin onboard. They were once harmonious crew members under the loving command of the Royal Captain. However, all except the little golden fish inhabited by the *living* spirit of the Chief Officer qualified, in their prevailing circumstance, as a true crew of the Royal Ship. The Leviathan and all the other species had severed relationship with their origin and were no longer qualified to be regarded as crew members until they had been literally re-humanized or reborn, not only in mentality but also in form.

That Jesus Christ temporarily appeared amongst us in our human form did not make his *living* Spirit of equal status with ours. He purposely assumed our present nature to be able to reach and communicate with us in our familiar human language. He also needed to confront the Leviathan of our situation face to face. The Scripture makes these facts explicit.

Hebrew 2:14-15 says, "Since therefore the children [of the Father now] share in flesh and blood, he [the living Christ] himself [voluntarily] partook of the same nature, that through [such temporary spiritual] death he might [come face to face and] destroy him who has [who wields] the power of death [in the world], that is, [Jehovah/Allah] the devil, and deliver all those who through fear of death were subjected to lifelong bondage." Then 1 John 3:8 added, "The reason the Son of the Father appeared [in human form] was to destroy the [oppressive] works of [Jehovah/Allah] the devil."

In the first phase of his rescue mission in the world, the heavenly Christ came in his true nature as redeeming Spirit of Knowledge, but human beings could not and did not recognize him. Only Adam and Eve were able to appreciate the central essence of his mission, and he commissioned their family lineage as *prophets* to disseminate information about his second coming in human form. Sons of Adam prophesied the expected second coming of the heavenly Messiah, while Jehovah/Allah relentlessly tried to infiltrate their ranks and to confuse their Good News messages.

Jehovah/Allah eventually succeeded in delving a near permanent breach in the prophetic heritage of Adam's family when he cunningly abducted and re-colonized **Abram.** Abram meant *"the Father is exalted,"* but Jehovah/Allah turned him into the materialistic **Abraham** of our present age, which meant the proxy *"father of many nations"* of lost spirits. Then, he systematically brainwashed and hardened the descendants of Abraham into adamant opposers of their coming friend and Messiah.

With the help of the re-colonized descendants of Abraham, Jehovah/Allah gradually metamorphosed from a mere homeless, easygoing, magic-working mountain hermit that Abraham adopted as family tutelary deity into the undisputed *God* of the whole universe. He now claims to be the only *God* in existence and even blindly attempting to impersonate the Father himself. He founded Judaism for the Jews, a religious cult of himself, to which he entrusted with spreading the lie that he is the only *God*.

Meanwhile, Jehovah/Allah branded the heavenly Spirit of Knowledge that enlightened and liberated Adam and Eve as serpent, devil, and an archenemy of humankind. He convinced the Jews that he had come from *nowhere* to destroy his "perfect" world and therefore, to deprive them of all the good things that he had prepared for them in the world. Sadly, his lies stock firmly in the minds of his Jewish captives, as well as in the minds of other blind followers of Abrahamic legacies.

No one desired to balance Jehovah/Allah's one-sided narrative by hearing or even imagining the sides of Adam, Eve and the one libeled as serpent. Of course, it was far easier for ignorant humans to believe the disgruntled god of Eden, because he spoke their language, and was ruthless and cunning enough to twist the truth in their feeble minds to his selfish advantage.

Nevertheless, the heavenly Spirit of Knowledge eventually appeared in human form in the person of Jesus Christ as prophesied by Adam and his sons. And as expected, he continued to enlighten and rekindle captive human spirits during his second coming as he did in Eden during his first coming. He specifically came as the lowliest of men so that people might feel free to come around him to hear his divine message of salvation for them. Indeed, dregs of society always gathered around him during his human ministry, and he taught them about the Father and what they must do as human beings to regain eternal life and their pride of place in the Father's glorious Kingdom.

The Scripture reports that:

"He went about all Galilee, teaching in their synagogues **and preaching the gospel of [return to] the Kingdom** and healing every disease and every infirmity among the people [that the wicked Jehovah/Allah had inflicted on them]. So, his fame spread throughout all Syria, and they brought him all the sick, those afflicted [by Jehovah/Allah] with various diseases and pains, demoniacs, epileptics, and paralytics, and he healed them. Great crowds followed him from Galilee and the Decapolis and Jerusalem and Judea and from beyond the Jordan." [Matthew 4:23-25]

"And they went into Capernaum; and immediately on the sabbath he entered the synagogue and taught. And they were astonished at his teaching, for **he taught them as one who had authority**, and not as the scribes [who were largely inspired by Jehovah/Allah, the impostor]." [Mark 1:21]

The second coming of the heavenly Spirit of Knowledge became a great success because people saw, touched, heard and talked directly with him. Although Jehovah/Allah and his human abettors publicly nailed his human cloak on the tree in Jerusalem, the present Eden, his fame and success have continued to grow and spread to all parts of the world. More than two thousand years after his gruesome crucifixion, no honest human being can possibly deny the fact that Jesus Christ has indeed, overcome the world. He overcame Jehovah/Allah, the supreme Leviathan of our present world of darkness in Eden during his first coming. He also overcame him and all his occult and human helpers in Jerusalem during his second coming. Accordingly, he authoritatively says, "I have overcome the world." [John 16:33]

The third phase of his salvation program is presently running and recording astounding successes too. This is the spirit harvesting or mopping up phase of the Holy Spirit of truth. The heavenly Christ now beams the Father's goodwill message directly to captive human spirits just as the Chief Officer beamed the Royal Captain's goodwill messages directly to the fallen crew.

It is an undeniable fact that many people in the world now know about our true heavenly Father and his divine mandate for the spiritual salvation of our fallen dead spirits more than ever before. We also know now that the Interim Paradise, the equivalent of the re-humanizing chamber in the Royal Ship analogy, is already teaming with multitudes of redeemed spirits, not just of Adam and the true prophets of Israel, but also of the so-called Gentiles.

Humans can now confidently testify that **Jesus Christ was indeed the only truly living Son of God the Father that ever came into this world of darkness**, for no one else has ever been as loving and kind to humanity as he. Thus, the Scripture says, "Therefore the Father has highly exalted him and bestowed on him the name which is above every name [ever known and worshiped by human beings], that at the name of Jesus [Christ, not Jehovah/Allah] every knee should bow, **in heaven and on earth and under the earth**, and every tongue confess that Jesus Christ [not Jehovah/Allah] is Lord [of our spiritual salvation], to the glory of the Father. [Philippians 2:9-11]

Finally, the first Epistle of John seals the testimony, saying, "And this is the testimony, that the Father gave us eternal life, and this life is [only attainable] in his Son. He who has the Son has life; he who has not the Son of the Father has not life. ... And we know that the Son of the Father has come and has given us understanding, to know him who is true; and we are in him who is true, in his Son Jesus Christ. This is our true Father and eternal life. ... "He who believes in the Son of the Father has the testimony in himself." [1 John 5:11-12, 20, 10]

The fourth and final phase of the mission of the heavenly Spirit of Knowledge will signal the Last Day of the ongoing spiritual Judgment or spirit harvest time. It would be the long proclaimed Great Day of Resurrection when Jesus Christ, as our *sole* Rescue Officer, would descend once more to finally gather, restore to full spiritual life, and present the entire occupants of the Interim Paradise to the Father's presence in his heavenly Kingdom. "Then the righteous will shine like the sun in the kingdom of their Father," says Matthew 13:43.

For all the redeemed, the gruesome memories of worldly existence will literally pass away, never to be remembered ever again. The Scripture says that "those who are accounted worthy to attain to that age and to the resurrection from the dead neither marry nor are given in marriage, for they cannot die anymore; because **they are equal to angels and are [once more bona fide] sons of the Father, being sons of the Resurrection.**" [Luke 20:35-36]

With the Great Day of Resurrection, there will be a total withdrawal of the Messiah's only line of communication with the world. That will signal the official termination of the Father's long period of grace. All forms of goodness and artificial lights in the world, both of ambience and of purity of purpose, will automatically cease. This illusory world as we now know it as human beings will completely disappear, thereby returning the situation to the primordial state of "perfect darkness, lifelessness, and void."

The unrepentant spirits of Jehovah/Allah and those who remained loyal to him will suddenly begin to experience the real agonizes of eternal death as fallen dead spirits in the overwhelming Outer Darkness. Matthew 25:30 says, "There men will weep and gnash their teeth." And John 3:19 explains that "This is [will be] the judgment, that the light has come into the world, and men loved darkness rather than light, because their deeds were evil."

JESUS CHRIST AS THE ONLY TRUE LIGHT THAT ENLIGHTENS EVERY MAN IN THE WORLD

The Quran says that "Allah is the Light of the heavens and the earth." But it also defines the light of Allah as a "dim lamp in a dark niche," found only in religious shines where beguiled religious believers worship him as *God Almighty*. "The similitude of His light," the Quran says, "is as a niche wherein is a lamp. The lamp is in a glass. The glass is as it were a shining star. (This lamp is) kindled from a Blessed Tree [of Light], an Olive neither of the East nor of the West [i.e. not of this world], whose oil would almost glow forth (of itself) though no fire touched it." ... "(This lamp [light of Allah] is found) in houses which Allah hath allowed to be exalted and that His name shall be remembered therein. Therein [beguiled religious believers] do offer praise to Him at morn and evening." [Quran 24:35-36]

So, Allah is just a corrupted light that was originally kindled from the Blessed Tree of Light. As we already know, the Father is Eternal Light. He is the Blessed Tree of Light and darkness has never had any place in him or in his Son Jesus Christ. That is why the Scripture says that "The light [Jesus Christ] shines in the darkness, and the darkness has not overcome it." [John 1:5]

Well, the Jewish Talmudic tradition has it that the "original light" of Jehovah/Allah was apparent within the worldly creation for just 36 hours before it went into hiding. Indeed, Jehovah/Allah "shined" in his Edenic paradise for only 3 days before the sudden advent of the heavenly Christ as true light into the world. Thereafter, darkness overcame him completely, and that was very remarkable indeed.

The Talmudic tradition blames Adam for scaring the original light of Jehovah/Allah into abrupt disappearance. It argues that Jehovah/Allah had depended on Adam to reveal his original light to the whole world, but he failed him. And because he could not shine his own light for everyone to see, he had to wait for a whole 2000 years for another man, a direct descendant of Adam, to help him to shine out from his dark niches. Luckily for him, the man, Abram, came along.

Pretending to be a friend, he coned and abducted Abram, altered his name and spiritual focus away from the true light, and then rejoiced for a while that through him the whole world would finally mistake him for the true light. Indeed, Abraham helped Jehovah to prepare the grounds, while Moses institutionalized his false hope in the Torah and Judaism. Eventually, the Jewish tradition started looking up to the Torah as the "hidden light" of Jehovah. But Jehovah/Allah never really shines in the world in any way that enlightened human beings can see and appreciate as true light. On the contrary, he seems to have sunken deeper into the darker niches of the world.

Evidently, Jehovah/Allah knew that the Jewish 'hidden light of the Torah' argument would not sustain his false position forever. His *hidden light* must somehow emerge from the Torah and diversify. He badly needed to keep up the story to buy as much time as he could. He needed other human redeemers to help keep his fake light shimmering, with yet other religious books to burrow into. Saul of Tarsus came to his rescue with the heavily interpolated *Christian Bible*, and Muhammad of Arabia followed closely with the Quran.

Then, Jehovah/Allah confirmed that Muhammad was the last bearer of his mysterious *hidden light*. "O People of the Scripture [Jews and customary Christians]! Now hath Our messenger come unto you, expounding unto you much of that which ye used to hide in the Scripture,… **Now hath come unto you Light from Allah and a plain Scripture**. Whereby Allah guideth him who seeketh His good pleasure unto paths of peace. He bringeth them out of darkness unto light by His decree, and guideth them unto a straight path… "O mankind! Now hath a proof from your Lord come unto you, and **We have sent down unto you a clear Light**. … "So, believe in Allah and His messenger and the light which We have revealed." [Quran 5:15-16; 4:174; 64:8]

So, Muhammad of Arabia is the final *hidden light* of Jehovah/Allah. This is quite remarkable and understandable. The footprint is already unmistakable all over the world. But it means that beyond Muhammad, Islam and the Quran, Jehovah/Allah has nowhere else to hide. This already puts him under immense nervous tension, which is why he is currently doubling down with radical Islamic terrorism all over the world.

From Abraham to Moses, to the Torah; from Saul of Tarsus to the heavily interpolated *Christian Bible*, and from Muhammad of Arabia to the Quran, yet the light of Jehovah/Allah remains the kind of light that shines only in thick darkness. All his hide-and-seek galimatias have yielded nothing good for true humanity but hardness of hearts, spiritual regression, bad leadership, radical Islamic terrorism, senseless wars, socioeconomic devastations, and deaths.

Anyway, the Bible concedes that Jehovah/Allah is "God of Darkness" and the chief custodian of the evil "treasures of darkness." According to 1 Kings 8:12, "Jehovah/Allah has set the sun in the heavens, but has said that he would [continue to] dwell in thick darkness." And he does. On one occasion during the

Jewish Exodus, Exodus 20:21 reported that "the people stood afar off, while **Moses drew near to the thick darkness where Jehovah/Allah was**." Jehovah/Allah himself once recruited Cyrus of Persia as his personal 'hammer of justice' and said to him, "**I will give you the treasures of darkness** and the hoards in secret places, that you may know that it is I, Jehovah, the God of Israel, who call you by your name." [Isaiah 45:3]

With Jehovah/Allah, the whole world remained in total darkness till the Father's Word of Life manifested in Eden as the Spirit of Knowledge and brought spiritual reawakening and the light of life into the world. The sons of Adam saw the true light and prophesied. Prophet Isaiah proclaimed that "The people who walked in darkness have seen a great light; those who dwelt in a land of deep darkness, on them has light shined." And while the world waited for the eventual Incarnation of the true light in human form, the true prophets of Israel continued to assure that "The true light that enlightens every man was coming into the world." [John 1:9]

At the appointed time, the true Light "became flesh and dwelt among us, full of grace and truth; we have beheld his glory, glory as of the only [living] Son from the Father." [John 1:14] Since then, the world has witnessed evolution in knowledge, goodness, and spiritual refinement. And as expected, Jesus Christ says, "I have come as light into the world, that whoever believes in me may not remain in darkness." ... "I am the light of the world; he who follows me will not walk in darkness, but will have the light of life." [John 12:46; 8:12]

But the true Light will not shine in this world of darkness forever. He is only here for the limited period of divine grace; to enlighten and to guide genuine seekers of spiritual rebirth back to the Father of Light, and back to their proper heavenly dwelling. Hence, Jesus Christ says, "As long as I am in the world, I am the light of the world." ... "The light is with you for a little longer. Walk while you have the light, lest the darkness overtake you [completely]; he who walks in the darkness does not know where he goes. While you have the light, believe in the light, that you may become sons of Light." [John 9:5; 12:35-36]

The heavenly Spirit of Knowledge became "the true light that enlightens every man" in the world. He has indeed been here with us for such a long time and has taught and impacted our lives in the most extraordinary, life-giving ways. The true gospel of Jesus Christ is the light and the life that the Father sent to us in the world. Jesus Christ affirmed that, saying, "It is the spirit that gives life, the flesh is of no avail; the words that I have spoken to you are spirit and life." John 6:63

Thus, the coming of the heavenly Christ into the world has automatically rendered Jehovah/Allah's claim of being 'the light of heavens and earth' null and void.

JESUS CHRIST IS TRUTH AND LIFE

As we already know, all the spirits that violated the heavenly norm of perfect existence were spewed from the realm of Divine Light and into the Outer Darkness. They all dwelt in total darkness as a matter of inevitability until the heavenly Christ ushered in a measure of divine light into their prison of darkness.

I am sure that people can appreciate the debilitating difficulties associated with total darkness by imagining a dark room laboratory, which is artificially created by excluding all possible sources of light. The primordial situation was far worse than a temporary dark laboratory, as the total absence of divine light meant both ambient and inner darkness for the fallen spirits. It meant extinction of their divine nature or simply spiritual death. Not even the subsequent invention of artificial lights of stars and moons could cancel out the darkness that overwhelmed the fallen dead spirits. That is why the Scripture maintains that "The world is a dark place, and its people have no light." [2 Esdras 14:20 (GNB)]

These simple truths have been turned upside down by Jehovah/Allah and his religious propagandists in a fruitless attempt to obscure knowledge of the uniqueness and authority of Jesus Christ as the true light of the world. The whole purpose of human religion is to perpetuate the false narratives of the Genesis creation fable that libeled the redeeming heavenly Christ as serpent and archenemy of humankind. Religion does not only market Jehovah/Allah as the sole creator of the universe but also as the light of world.

The Quran says that Jehovah/Allah "is the light of the heavens and the earth," and "the Protecting Friend of those who believe [in him]. **He bringeth them out of darkness into light**." [Quran 24:35; 2:257] That is a sheer paradox for a god that the Bible affirms that he continues to dwell in thick darkness by choice. 1 Kings 8:12 says that he himself "has said that he would continue to dwell in thick darkness." And Psalms 18:11(NIV) says that "He made darkness his covering, his canopy around him."

There are two main reasons Jehovah/Allah prefers dwelling in darkness. First, his deeds are evil. And second, darkness offers him needed camouflage to draw ignorant humans into his comfort zone to keep them away from the true light and to prevent them from knowing the whole truth. But the true light has shown himself to the whole world in ways that Jehovah/Allah never did and can never do, and the difference is already crystal clear to every clear-thinking mind on earth. "For this I have come into the world," says the heavenly Christ, "to bear witness to the truth." [John 18:37] There is no doubt that Christ's gospel of truth and life has taken root and is already permeating every nook and cranny of the inhabited world.

Jesus Christ had promised to speak to humans directly and in plain words about the Father and his gracious offer in the later days. "I have yet many things to say to you, but you cannot bear them now [then]," he said. "When the Spirit of truth comes, he will guide you into all the truth; ... "I have said this to you in figure; **the hour is coming when I shall no longer speak to you in figures but tell you plainly of the Father.**" [John 16:12, 25] We are now living in the said later days. The final stages of the spirits' harvest phase of the Messiah's redemptive mission are already here with us. And the whole world is now experiencing unprecedented spiritual reawakening.

Jesus Christ meant that in these later days, the Spirit of truth from the Father will explain his true gospel directly to all his true disciples in the world irrespective of their tribes, class, creed or ordination. "It is written in the prophets," says Jesus Christ, 'They shall all be taught by the Father.' And "Everyone who has heard and learned from the Father will come to me." [John 6:45] Modern-day gospel racketeers who monopoly the gospel of Jesus Christ on the grounds of worldly ordinations should know that they are not recognized.

This is the time that every true disciple of Jesus Christ, people to whom he has revealed himself and his Father, must explain the gospel of the true Kingdom plainly to others. Any reader who has carefully followed the foregoing discourse would have understood how Jesus Christ is the only Son of our truly loving Father in the world. He would equally be in a good position to understand how he is also the only true light that enlightens every man in the world. However, we still need to sharpen our perspective with the Royal Ship analogy from time to time.

Before we proceed further, it is very important to correct the wrong interpretation that Jehovah's apostles give to the Divine Incarnation of the Father's "Word of Life" into the world. We read in John 3:16 that the Father "willed" to grant eternal life to all his fallen dead sons in the Outer Darkness because he still loved them so much. The same verse also tells us that the Father "sent" his living Son, Jesus Christ into the word as the physical manifestation of his spoken "Word of Life." It is evident from the verse that the world of the fallen *dead* spirits existed outside the heavenly domain of the Father and his *living* Son. As a nation does not send an envoy to itself, Jesus Christ was the Father's sole official "Envoy" to the world.

Talking about the Father's Word of Life that incarnated into the world, John 1:1 says, "In the beginning was the Word, and the Word was with the Father, and the Word was the Father [himself]." This verse clearly talks about the formative stage of the Father's divine initiative as regards his will to send a Rescue Officer to his fallen dead sons in the world. It is specifically intended to stress the Father's oneness with Jesus Christ who became the physical incarnation of his "Word of Life" in the world. Jesus Christ reiterated the intended message of this very verse when he said in John 10:30, "I and my Father are one."

But Jehovah's apostles deliberately interpolated verses 2 and 3 into the text in a baseless attempt to link the Father and his Son to the fictitious creation of our world of darkness. John 1:2-3 reads, "He was in the beginning with God; all things were made through him, and without him was not anything made that was made." These two verses speak about the creation of the world and not about salvation of fallen dead spirits in the world. The two verses are entirely unconnected with the Father's "Word of Life" that came into the world that already existed to give life to spirits that had already sinned, fallen and died.

The sinful spirits had already been spewed out of the heavenly Kingdom of the Father and they had already invented their makeshift physical world of darkness before the commencement of the Father's rescue initiative. It could not have been otherwise. Someone has first to fall into the water before the rescuer would arrange for his rescue. Likewise, someone must first be dead before any plan for his resurrection can become necessary. The Father's Word of Life was not sent into the world to create it, it was sent to rescue fallen dead spirits trapped in it.

So, the 'beginning' mentioned in John 1:1 does not refer to the beginning of our imperfect physical world, but to the beginning of the Father's rescue initiative for his lost sons in the world. Sadly, Jehovah/Allah's religious propagandists deliberately explain that *spiritual beginning* of the process of Divine Incarnation of the Father's Word of Life as referring to the *physical beginning* of the clumsy efforts of the groping dead spirits at making a material world for themselves.

The true meaning of John 1:1 will become more obvious to anyone who reads the full text from verse 1-18. Certainly, the Father did not speak his Word of Life into the Outer Darkness to create a world, but he sent him to redeem fallen dead spirits that were already in an existing world. Jesus Christ of Nazareth became the physical manifestation of the Father's *spiritual* Will or Word of Life in the world. John tried to capture the sheer miracle of the Divine Incarnation of the heavenly Christ in that simple verse, but Jehovah's apostles present a totally false narrative. The Divine Incarnation of Jesus Christ conveys the Father's ultimate assurance that whoever receives his Son in the world will surely live again, just as the Son lives.

As we already know, the Father is Spirit, so his Will to rescue his lost sons in the world could only leave him as Spiritual Energy. Before the fall of the rebellious spirits, that Spiritual Energy was in the Father, and it was indeed the Father himself. That Spiritual Energy from the Father first appeared in Eden to the fallen dead spirits of Adam and Eve and assured them that they would live again. The rest of humankind did not see or perceive him because in their corrupted nature they could not see or perceive spiritual manifestation.

The same Spiritual Energy from the Father later incarnated on earth amongst Adam's descendants in the person of Jesus Christ of Nazareth and we saw, touched and talked with him. In fact, we literally saw, touched and talked with the Father himself. That was a great miracle indeed! That was why Jesus Christ could say, "I and the Father are one." [And] "He who has seen me has seen the Father." [John 10:30; 14:9]

The Father is eternal Light and Light is Life. The Father's Word of Life is eternal Life indeed. So, by saying that "*the Word is the Father*," John meant that "*the Eternal Life he was sending into the world is the Father himself*." There is really no ambiguity in that.

John's perfect testimony thus goes like this: "And the Word [the spiritual life-giving Energy from the Father] became flesh and dwelt among us, full of grace and truth; we have beheld his glory, glory as of the only Son from the Father. ... "That which was from the beginning, **which we have heard** [from the mouth of the true prophets of Israel], which we have seen with our eyes, which we have looked upon and touched with our hands, **concerning the [Father's] Word of Life**—the Life was made manifest, and we saw it, and testify to it, and proclaim to you *the eternal Life which was with the Father* and was made manifest to us— ... And this is the testimony, that **the Father gave us eternal Life**, and **this Life is in his Son**." [John 1:14; 1 John 1:1-2; 5:11]

We now know the true meaning of the "Word" in John 1:1. People should also want to know, "at what precise point during the creation of our imperfect world did the Father's Word of Life first manifest into it?" Certainly, not when the groping spirits that were caught up in primordial darkness were invoking into existence false lights of stars and moons that did not give life. Neither was it when Jehovah/Allah formed his zoo paradise in Eden, held Adam and Eve as captives in it and banned knowledge of good and evil for humankind. From the beginning to the end of the so-called creation, the world represented terminal opposition to the Father's Will or Word of Life. Nothing about the created world, even slightly, portrayed existence or involvement of Divine Light or the Father's Word of Life.

The *first coming* of the Father's Word of Life into the world was as the redeeming Spirit of Knowledge in Eden. It made sense that the Father's Word of Life first came to open the inner eyes of captives who were maliciously kept in the dark about true light and life. Even then, the world and its Gods did not embrace the Father's Word of Life. And they have continued to oppose him by working tirelessly to re-blindfold enlightened humans.

The first coming of the redeeming Spirit of Knowledge in Eden marked the "beginning" of the mission of the Father's Word of Life in the world. It indicated the physical starting point of the Father's spiritual salvation program for captive human spirits. So, the Father's Word of Life says nothing about creation of the world but rather echoes the Father's Divine Will to make us live again.

The very *beginning* of the mission of the Father's Word of Life in the hostile world should be the precise point in the history of the world when the Father's special Envoy made the positive promise of eternal life to human beings on earth. "**You will not die**," was the opening statement of the Father's Word of Life to humankind in Eden. It was the Father's inviolable Divine Reassurance of eternal life to every fallen dead spirit in the world that receives his *only* Son, Jesus Christ. Evidently, this "beginning" has nothing whatsoever to do with the "beginning of invention" of the world of darkness, which in fact, poses great obstacle to the divine mission of the heavenly Christ.

That precise point in time occurred not at the beginning of the fictitious creation of the world but in the so-called Garden of Eden, when the Father's Word of Life descended for the first time and relayed the Father's Divine promise of life to humankind through Adam's family. The redeeming Spirit of Knowledge stated the Father's unchanged Will explicitly, saying to humankind, "**You will not die**. For Jehovah [god of the world] knows that when you eat of it [of the Word or Fruit of Knowledge] your [spiritual] eyes will be opened, and you will be like *God*, knowing good and evil." [Genesis 3:4] Without that it would have been impossible for humans to see the true light or aspire to reach the Blessed Tree of life.

The eye-opening encounter that Adam and Eve had with the Father's Word of Life in Eden exactly signaled the beginning of the first phase of the Messiah's redemptive mission in the world. It was at that point that the Father's Word of Life commissioned Adam's family as his prophetic forerunners, to inform the rest of humankind about his subsequent incarnation. Incarnation of the Father's Word of Life will mark his *second coming* into the world and represent the practical phase of his redemptive mission.

The Scripture affirmed that Adam and Eve ate of the fruit of the Father's Word of Life in Eden and "Then the [spiritual] eyes of both were opened, and they knew that they were naked; **and they sewed fig leaves together and made themselves aprons [of morality]**." [Genesis 3:7] That represented the first direct outcome of the Father's glorious intervention in the affairs of worldly beings. Expectedly, Jehovah/Allah, god of Eden, libeled the Father's life-giving Word serpent and devil, and blinded religious believers agree with him even to this day.

The Father's Word of Life eventually incarnated as prophesied, and he was none other than Jesus Christ of Nazareth. He became the Father's *sole* Envoy to the world, and the *only* true Messiah for captive human spirits. As expected, the world has never been the same since the heavenly Christ walked the earth in human form. He has made an unmistakable impact on the normal course of the world. His first coming ushered in the knowledge of good and evil, functional mind, conscience, and common sense, while his second coming invigorated humankind's evolution in knowledge, goodness, and spiritual refinement.

On the contrary, the coming of the Father's Word of Life into the world marked the beginning of Jehovah/Allah's terminal indignation against awakened humankind, and his interminable shadowboxing against the redemptive mission of the Word in the world. He could not even disguise his feelings of humiliation, frustration, and downright opposition to the gracious will of the Father. He confessed that enlightened humans now have direct access to the Father who is Eternal Life, and he vowed to hinder them. "Now the man has become like one of us and has knowledge of what is good and what is bad," he said. ... "Then at the east side of the garden he put living creatures and a flaming sword which turned in all directions. **This was to keep [prevent] anyone from coming near the tree that gives life**." [Genesis 3:22, 24 (GNB)]

Jehovah/Allah's opposition to the Father's Word of Life for humankind commenced on that fateful day in Eden and will climax with his expected "tribulations of the last days." He confessed that everything was going as he had planned in the world before the Father's Word of Life stepped into it. The same *God* who, according to Genesis 1:31, "saw everything that he had made, and behold, it was very good," was suddenly said in Genesis 6:6 to be "sorry that he had made man on the earth, and it grieved him to his heart." He was clearly a frustrated impostor. Evidently, he did not know what the future would be because he was not omniscient.

According to 2 Esdras 9:18-21(GNB), he lamented, saying, "Before I created this world or the people who would live in it, no one opposed me, because no one existed [that could oppose me from within the world]. When I had created the world, I supplied it with an abundance of food and a Law of profound wisdom, but the people I created lived corrupt lives. I looked at my world and saw that it was ruined. **I saw that my earth was in danger of being destroyed by the wicked plans of the people [the Messiah] who had come into it**. When I saw this, I found it very difficult to spare them, ..." Surely, Jehovah/Allah did not sound like a true divine being who had absolute control over the world of which he claimed to be the sole creator.

He merely branded the Father's Word of Life as serpent and devil, just to deviate attention from himself who was the real venomous snake. Then, he swore to permanently afflict enlightened humankind with suffering and physical death and to set them at enmity with their true heavenly Redeemer. "Jehovah *God* said to *the serpent* [i.e. the Father's Word of Life], because you have done this [because you have promised the people eternal life], ... I will put enmity between you and the woman, and between your seed [of spiritual enlightenment] and her seed [which is humanity in general]." [Genesis 3:15]

To this day, Jehovah/Allah continues to swear vengeance, while endlessly trying to return enlightened humankind to the original mold of terminal ignorance in Eden. He swears, "I will take vengeance, and I will spare no man. ... "Return to me and be saved [from my jealous rage], all the ends of the earth! For I am *God*, and there is no other. By myself I have sworn, from my mouth has gone forth ... a word that shall not return: '**To me every knee shall bow, every tongue shall swear.**' ... And "As I live, says Jehovah *God*, surely with a mighty hand and an outstretched arm, and **with wrath poured out, I will be king over you.**" [Isaiah 47:3; 45:22-23; Ezekiel 20:33] These are all but the angry outburst of a humiliated, shortsighted and adamant evil spirit.

Becoming a king over ignorant human beings on earth is all that Jehovah/Allah aspires to. But truly enlightened humans seek outright spiritual resurrection of their captive spirits from the entire spheres of the world of darkness. People who still see the world as a creation of the Father will remain overshadowed by the will of Jehovah/Allah. They will continue to misapprehend the true "beginning" of the mission of the Father's Word of Life in the world. That is why the Scripture counsels, "Do not be conformed to this world but be transformed by the renewal of your mind, **that you may prove what is the [actual] Will of [our true heavenly Father]**, what is good and acceptable and perfect [for the spiritual resurrection]." [Romans 12:2]

In fact, the Scripture draws a definite battle line between the world and the Father's Incarnate Will or Word of Life. James 4:4 says that "friendship with the world is enmity with the Father," that "whoever wishes to be a friend of the world [or friend of Jehovah/Allah, god of the world] makes himself an enemy of the Father." Hence, 1 John 2:15-17 added, "Do not love the world or the things in the world. If anyone loves the world [or Jehovah/Allah, god of the world], love for the Father is not in him. For all that is in the world, the lust of the flesh and the lust of the yes and the pride of [this] life, is not of the Father but is of the world. And the world [certainly] passes away, with the lust of it; but he who does the Will of the Father abides forever."

In his book, *The Aristos*, John Fowles presents his own understanding of the "beginning" as it relates to John 1:1 and vis-à-vis the Genesis account of creation of the imperfect world of humans. He perceived a sudden emergence of an overriding Sovereign Authority into the world that created the onset of humankind's spiritual evolution but was not associated with the creation of the imperfect world itself. He read the Genesis account of the so-called "Fall of Adam" not as a fall but as humankind's sudden "Move" toward genuine spiritual growth:

> "I interpret the myth of the temptations of Adam in this way: **Adam** [the way Jehovah/Allah had programmed him] is hatred of change and futile nostalgia for the innocence of animals; **the Serpent** [or the Divine Spirit of Knowledge] is imagination, the power to compare, self-consciousness; **Eve** is the assumption of human responsibility, of the need for progress and the need to control progress; **the Garden of Eden** is an impossible dream [by Jehovah/Allah], a Parahades of the past; **the Fall** is the essential *processus* of [humankind's spiritual] evolution, and would be much better termed **the Move. The God of Genesis** [Jehovah/Allah] is a personification [the implanter] of Adam's resentment." [John Fowles; Aristos, page 68:12]

From this general overview of the subject matter, we can now begin to understand why the Scripture refers to Jesus Christ as the true light that enlightens every man in this world of darkness. This clearly suggests the presence of a "false light" that deliberately deceives and leads human beings astray. The "true light" stands for the truth, while "false light" stands for falsehood, for deliberate misinformation. "True Light" has absolutely nothing to do with artificial lights of the stars, moons, or electricity, but refers to the Divine Source of truth and life. It refers to spiritual insight that guarantees outright spiritual emancipation and ascent of captive human spirits.

Applying these known facts to the issue of the Father's Will for our spiritual salvation, one can easily see that Jesus Christ is the only true source of genuine information, while Jehovah/Allah stands diametrically opposed to the Father's Word of Life. Jesus Christ is literally "the Truth" and "the Way" and "the Life" that our captive spirits earnestly yearn for. Jehovah/Allah, on the contrary, is "the father of lies," and "the deceiver of the whole world." He lies, even when he seems to be telling the truth, and his utterances and actions consistently portray his express desire.

The scriptures are equally very clear on this. The Quran says that "Allah verily sendeth whom he will astray," and then asks, "Are they [human beings] then secure from Allah's scheme? None deemeth himself secure from Allah's scheme save folks that perish. ... "He whom **Allah sendeth astray**, for him there is no protecting friend after Him." [Quran 35:8; 7:99; 42:44] Indeed, Allah confesses that he could tell human beings the truth but that his real desire is to lead them all astray. "And if We had so willed, We could have given every spirit its [truthful] guidance," he says, "but the word from Me ... took effect: that **I will fill hell with the jinn and mankind together**." [Quran 32:13]

The Bible, on its part, says that Jehovah/Allah deliberately casts spell of deep sleep on people. His evil mantra on humankind reads: "Stupefy yourselves and be in a stupor, blind yourselves and be blind! Be drunk, but not with wine; stagger, but not with strong drink! For **Jehovah has poured out upon you a spirit of deep sleep, and has closed your eyes**, the seer. ... "so that they may indeed see but not perceive, and may indeed hear but not understand." [Isaiah 29:9-10 and Mark 4:12]

Furthermore, Jehovah/Allah himself admits that he deliberately gives people laws that do not give life. "Moreover," he says in Ezekiel 20:25, "**I gave them [the Jews] statutes that were not good and ordinances by which they could not have life**; and I defiled them through their very gifts in making them offer by fire all their first-born, that I might horrify them; I did it that they might know that I am Jehovah." There are really no ambiguities in the words of these scriptures.

JESUS CHRIST AS THE ONLY WAY TO THE TREE OF LIFE

The Father's Word of Life, spoken for all the fallen dead spirits in the world, is the only link at present, between the Father and this world of darkness. Jesus Christ is the spiritual and physical manifestation of that Word in the world. As the diagram on page 11 shows, the narrow line of brightness between the Father's glorious abode and our present nether world of darkness represents the only possible way back to the realm of eternal life. Jesus Christ represents that way exclusively. Hence he authoritatively says, "I am the Way, and the Truth, and the Life; no one comes to the Father, but by me." [John 14:6]

However, for people to appreciate the unique position of Jesus Christ as the only way back to the heavenly Kingdom of the Father, it is necessary for us to go back to the very first coming of the Spirit of the Word in Eden. Even though Jehovah/Allah had maligned the Divine Spirit of Knowledge and Life that appeared to Adam and Eve as serpent and devil, the facts say otherwise. Clear-thinking human beings are now able to re-evaluate the fateful incident in Eden without the habitual religious bias to arrive at the truth.

It is most important to focus on the actual words and accomplishments of the alleged serpent. Jehovah/Allah had forbidden spiritual enlightenment for humankind and threatened that knowledge would cause us to die. But the Father's Redeeming Word of Life assured humankind that that was a wicked lie. "For Jehovah/Allah knows that when you eat of it your eyes will be opened, and you will be like God, knowing good and evil," he said. [Genesis 3:5] His authoritative word of honor to humankind was **"You will not die!"**

The Father's Word of Life in Eden convinced Adam and Eve that 'knowledge gives life and not death,' and he encouraged them to imbibe spiritual enlightenment. Indeed, when Adam and Eve imbibed his divine word of life, their spiritual eyes opened, and they saw clearly the way that led straight to the Blessed Tree of Life. They immediately took positive steps toward spiritual refinement, and thereby inaugurated humankind's spiritual evolution toward total spiritual emancipation.

It was obvious, therefore, that the alleged *Serpent* in Eden stood for humankind's spiritual enlightenment and ultimate resurrection to true eternal life. Jehovah/Allah on his part, openly opposed the divine will of the Father. He tried his utmost to obstruct the way to the Father who is the Blessed Tree of Life. "Then at the east side of the garden," says Genesis 3:24 (GNB), "he [Jehovah/Allah] put living creatures and a flaming sword which turned in all directions. [And] **This was to keep [prevent] anyone from coming near [the Father] the tree that gives life."**

When the Father's Word of Life incarnated as Jesus Christ, as Adam and his descendants had prophesied, he practically continued precisely where the redeeming *Serpent* had stopped. The core disagreement between the redeeming *Serpent* in Eden and Jehovah/Allah, the devious god of Eden, centered on the way back to the Tree of Life. While Jesus Christ promises to lead humankind to the Tree of Life, Jehovah/Allah forbids the Tree of Life for humankind and swears to "fill hell with the jinn and mankind together."

Jesus Christ says to the whole world that he is the *only* true way to the *forbidden* Tree of Life. In fact, he makes it emphatic that he and Jehovah/Allah are directly opposed to one another on the crucial issue of humankind's spiritual salvation. According to the prophesied details of the divine mission of the heavenly Christ in the world, the Father sent him specifically for the redemption and resurrection of fallen dead spirits. The Father sent him "to preach [the] good news [of eternal life] to the poor; to proclaim [eternal] release to the captives **and recovering of sight to the blind**; to set at liberty those who are oppressed and, to proclaim the acceptable year of the Father." [Luke 4:18-19]

There is no doubt that the divine mission of Jesus Christ corresponds to the unique initiatives of the redeeming *Serpent* in Eden. There would have been no need to stress the uniqueness of Jesus Christ and his divine mission if there were no concerted opposition to the Father's Will in the world. It became particularly necessary to qualify and distinguish Jesus Christ of Nazareth as "the only Son of the Father," "the only true light," "the resurrection and life" and "the only true way" back to the Father, because Jehovah/Allah craftily makes himself the false version of everything that the Messiah is. Jehovah/Allah is both Antichrist and false God Almighty in very sneaky ways. And through his various hypnotic religions of falsehood, he has successfully held almost the entire humankind spellbound even to this day.

The gospel truth, however, is that there are only two ways open to all fallen dead spirits in the world. The *way of light* that leads to spiritual life eternal in the Father's glorious Kingdom and the *way of darkness* that ultimately leads to *second* eternal death in the Outer Darkness. Jesus Christ refers to them as the *narrow way* and the *broad way*. Jesus Christ represents the **way of light** that leads to eternal life; hence he says, "I came that they [fallen dead spirits] may have life and have it abundantly." [John 10:10]

Jehovah/Allah, on the other hand, is the son of perdition that holds the keys of death and hades. He represents the **way of darkness** that leads to *second* eternal death.

Jehovah/Allah is the tree of Zaqqum, which symbolizes the tree of eternal death. He is not only the obstructer of the way of light; he is also the way of darkness that leads directly to eternal perdition. Although some of his religious ideologies may seem plausible to ignorant believers, they are all crafted to lead captive human spirits to the *second* eternal death. He says so himself. "And the word from Me ... took effect: that **I will fill hell with the jinn and mankind together**," he says. [Quran 32:13]

As we all know, every customary religion of this world has its mystical or cultic faction. In a desperate desire to access the so-called "treasures of darkness," greedy and overambitious worshipers usually end up as blind mystics. They blindly practice some weird and shameful rituals or religious practices that are commanded by Jehovah/Allah, all in the hope of achieving automatic ascent to the false heavens of the chief custodian of this present darkness. These blinded mystics are fooled by the false impression of ascending into heaven, but they are clearly trekking the way of darkness that leads to death. Their fate is the ultimate descent into eternal perdition in the Outer Darkness at the last day.

The people who chose Jehovah/Allah's way of darkness would have been self-condemned in the end. For, though the true light had come into the world, they had loved and chosen *the way of darkness* rather than *the way of light*. Some of these religious night marauders are given the impression of having ascended to the third heaven, to the seventh, to the thirteenth etc. Yet, standing at the apex of every Jacob-Ladder ascent is still the same Consuming One that has expressly vowed to *fill hell with the jinn and mankind together*.

The Scripture affirms that "he [Jacob] dreamed that there was a ladder set up on the earth, and the top of it reached to heaven; and behold, the [false] angels of God were ascending and descending on it! And behold, **Jehovah stood above it**." [Genesis 28:12-13] Also, referring to Quranic revelations, archangel Gabriel says in Quran 97:1-4, "Lo! We revealed it on the **Night of Power**. Ah, what will convey unto thee what the Night of Power is! The Night of Power is better than a thousand months. The [false] angels and the Spirit [of the so-called archangels] descend therein, by the permission of their Lord with all decrees." The way of darkness is always the way of midnight hours. And blind mystics understand why archangel Gabriel says that "The **Night of Power** is better than a thousand months."

The gospel truth, however, is that there is an unbridgeable chasm between the Father's heavenly Kingdom and our present world of darkness, between the true Heaven and Jehovah/Allah's mystical orb. The perfect spiritual Kingdom of the Father is a homogenous glorious realm of perfect existence for *only* perfect spirits. Fallen angels, archangels, and blind mystics do not ascend and descend from the true heavenly domain of the Father with Jacob ladders, and certainly, there is no night rendezvous there. Such ascents are merely illusory. In fact, Jesus Christ asserts that "No one has ever gone up to heaven except the Son of Man, who came down from heaven." [John 3:13(TEV)]

The *Way* of Jesus Christ is the *true way* to the Father's heavenly Kingdom, the way to the heavenly household of perfect living spirits, the way of love and perfect existence. Jesus Christ is the only *Way* that guarantees to lead every genuine seeker of spiritual salvation back to the Father, and therefore, back to his *proper* dwelling place among the true sons of Light. Accordingly, he says, "I am the way, and the truth, and the life; **no one comes to the Father, but by me**." [John 14:6] Indeed, since he alone came from the true glorious Heaven, only he can take us there.

Jesus Christ makes it clear that the Father is Love and that those who genuinely aspire to regain their full spiritual heritage in him must seek to be perfected in love. While Jehovah/Allah says that we "should love our neighbors and hate our enemies," Jesus

Christ says to us "Love your enemies and pray for those who persecute you, **so that you may be sons of your Father who is in heaven**; for he makes his sun rise on the evil and on the good, and sends rain on the just and on the unjust. ... You, therefore, must be perfect, as your heavenly Father is perfect." [Matthew 5:43-48]

In fact, love is the principal essence of the true gospel of Jesus Christ. And the golden rule is **"As you wish that men would do to you, do so to them."** [Luke 6:31] Numerous verses of the Scripture capture and further buttress the importance of love, and the inevitability of learning how to love for anyone who genuinely embraces the way of life:

- "So, we know and believe the love the Father has for us. The Father is love, and he who abides in love abides in the Father, and the Father abides in him. ... If anyone says, 'I love the Father,' and hates his brother, he is a liar; for he who does not love his brother whom he has seen, cannot love the Father whom he has not seen. And this commandment we have from him, that **he who loves the Father should love his brother also.**" [1 John 4:16, 20-21]

- "But love your enemies, and do good, and lend, expecting nothing in return; and your reward will be great, and you will be sons of the Most High; for he is kind to the ungrateful and the selfish. **Be merciful, even as your Father is merciful.**" [Luke 6:35-36]

- "Let love be genuine; hate what is evil, hold fast to what is good; love one another with brotherly affection; outdo one another in showing honor. ... Bless those who persecute you; bless and do not curse them. ... Repay no one evil for evil, but take thought for what is noble in the sight of all. If possible, so far as it depends upon you, live peaceably with all. ... 'if your enemy is hungry, feed him; if he is thirsty, give him drink; ... **Do not be overcome by evil, but overcome evil with good.**" [Romans 12:9-21]

- "Love is patience and kind; **love is not jealous** or boastful; it is not arrogant or rude. Love does not insist on its own way; it is not irritable or resentful; it does not rejoice at wrong, but rejoices in the right. Love bears all things, believes all things, hopes all things, endures all things. **Love never ends**; ..." [1 Corinthians 1:4-8]

Finally, all customary religions of the world preach love in various ways. They preach the Way of Jesus Christ because they know that it represents the ideal. Yet they inwardly uphold and practice the way of Jehovah/Allah, which is strictly the way of the world. Their prayers and songs of praises reflect nothing but vainglory and violence.

Indeed, it is practically impossible for any human being to practice in full the Way of Heaven here on earth because of the concerted opposition by the world. Nevertheless, genuine seekers of true heavenly life must persevere in reaching the ideal. Luckily people will not have to walk the whole distance home because the Father meets every true seeker midway, as in the case of the proverbial prodigal son.

JESUS CHRIST, THE INTERIM PARADISE AND THE ULTIMATE RESURRECTION

The most misinterpreted aspect of the gospel of Jesus Christ is the Paradise. Ordinarily, the word paradise means a place or state of bliss, felicity, or delight. Most customary religions of the world think of it as a final state or place of absolute bliss. In some customary religions of the world, the paradise is simply taken to mean "heaven" or the direct opposite of "hell."

Most often than not, religious believers take for granted the true meanings of "heaven" and "hell." They simply regard heaven as a picturesque, Eden-like Garden abode of the God of the world where righteous people proceed to after death, while hell is a nether region for the devil and demons, where dead sinners will be tormented forever.

Buddhists seek heaven or paradise as the final beatitude that transcends suffering, karma, and *samsara* [the endless reincarnation or transmigration of fallen spirits on earth]. They regard it as a place or state of oblivion to pain, care, or external reality.

Blind mystics, on their part, see haven as the nebulous orb, as some prophets of Israel described in the Torah, where Jehovah/Allah sits on a fiery throne that is surrounded by mundane earthly paraphernalia while receiving worship from all manners of imaginary creatures. The end goal of every mystic in all customary religions of the world is the "unification with the God of the world." To them, that also means paradise.

For instance, when an Eckankar minister speaks of their members ascending and descending from heaven on daily basis, he means that his sect has perfected the mystical formula of astral travel, and that people who desire to pay casual visits to the God of the world in his heaven or paradise readily do so. This agrees completely with the documented position of the mystical factions of Judaism, customary Christianity and Islam.

Heaven or Jannah means 'Garden' in Arabic. So, in Islam, heaven or paradise is imagined as an earthly "Garden of Pleasure" with lush greenery and flowing water. They believe that Muslim faithfuls will dwell there forever in grandeur and luxury; dressed in embroidered clothing, while reclining, eating, and drinking in the company of women. The Quran is full of verses speaking of **"gardens underneath which rivers flow"** as Allah's ultimate reward for those who help him in this life, in his futile battle against Jesus Christ and his redemptive mission in the world. Paradise is even called "**Gardens of Eden**" in the Quran.

"Verily Allah helpeth one who helpeth Him," says the Quran. ... "The reward of such will be forgiveness from their Lord, and *Garden underneath which rivers flow*, wherein they will abide for ever—a bountiful reward for **workers**! ... "Those who believe and do good works, them verily We shall house in lofty dwellings of the *Garden underneath which rivers flow*. There they will dwell secure. How sweet the guerdon [reward] of the **toilers**. ... "**Allah promiseth** to the believers, men and women, *Gardens underneath which rivers flow*, wherein they will abide—**blessed dwellings in Gardens of Eden.**" [Quran 22:40; 3:136; 29:58; 9:72]

As we all already know, Jehovah/Allah merely regards and uses Muslims as his expendable "slaves," "workers," and "toilers." So, believing that Allah's paradise would be exactly as the Quran describes it for Muslims is perhaps the weirdest fantasy of Islamic belief system. If the happiness, peace of mind, and life of Muslims mean nothing to Allah in this life, how could any clear-thinking Muslim expect that they would mean anything to him in the hereafter?

Incidentally, the Islamic view of paradise agrees with the Jewish hope in the *refurbished* earthly Gardens of the "New Jerusalem" that Jehovah promises them in the Torah. Of course, the present Jerusalem sits on the exact geographical location of the defunct Garden of Eden. But he promises them that "the former things shall not be remembered or come into mind," just as he successfully made us all to forget or overlook obvious details about the old Garden of Eden that still live with us to this day. [Isaiah 65:17]

Customary Christians are equally waiting for Jehovah's imaginary New Jerusalem, where he says that "The wolf also shall dwell with the lamb, the leopard shall lie down with the young goat, the calf and the young lion and the fatling together; and a little child shall lead them. The cow and the bear shall graze; their young ones shall lie down together; and the lion shall eat straw like the ox. The nursing child shall play by the cobra's hole, and the weaned child shall put his hand in the viper's den." [Isaiah 11:6-8(NKJV)]

It is also said that in Jehovah's expected utopian New Jerusalem, "Babies will no longer die in infancy, and all **people will live out their life span**. Those who live to be a hundred will be considered young. **To die before that would be a sign that I [Jehovah] had punished them**." [Isaiah 65:20-21(GNT)] So, we know that curses and death would remain irradicable aspects of life in Jehovah's so-called New Jerusalem. But though these crucial details are antithetical to their fundamental idea of a paradise, customary Christians still look forward to the sham.

Some Christians also picture paradise as a place of rest and refreshment where all righteous people who died on earth are *presently* basking in the glorious presence of *God*.

It is obvious from all the above notions that none of the customary religions of the world even has the slightest understanding of the true meaning of the Paradise, as it concerns the spiritual salvation of humankind. It is not surprising that Judaism and its proxy offshoots naturally use the word paradise as a synonym of the Garden of Eden before the so-called fall of Adam and Eve. Thus, they are all really waiting for the refurbished Garden of Eden that Jehovah/Allah promises his unsuspecting devotees.

All the customary religions of the world believe and teach that Jehovah/Allah, the god of the world, created the earth a paradise for human beings in the beginning, but that Adam and Eve singlehandedly ruined that. They, therefore, believe that since he created it in the beginning that he would do it again at the end, as he promises the various sects. So-called Christians who ought to know better are even the worst in the dark about this issue. By believing that the Paradise is a place "where **righteous dead people** *presently* **enjoy the glorious presence of God,**" they prove beyond doubt that they do not really know the Father or the Christ.

Jesus Christ is the sole guarantor of resurrection and life to all fallen dead spirits in the world; and he has made it emphatic that he would raise the saved spirits up *only* at the last day. No redeemed spirit can see or be able to appear in the presence of the Father until after the ultimate resurrection by Jesus Christ at the last day. And even their own Scripture says so plainly. "No one has ascended into heaven but he who descended from heaven, the Son of man," says Jesus Christ. ... And "Not that anyone has seen the Father except him who is from the Father; he has seen the Father." [John 3:13; 6:46]

The Jehovah's Witnesses sect is even far more conspicuous in their blinded expectation of Jehovah/Allah's *New Paradise* on earth. Evidently, they hope to remain mortal human beings on earth at the last day when Jesus Christ would have escorted all the redeemed spirits back to the Father's glorious Kingdom in their perfect spiritual nature. "For they cannot die anymore;" he assures, "because **they are equal to angels** [spirits] and are sons of the Father, being sons of the [Christ's] resurrection." [Luke 20:36]

The gospel truth is that there is no paradise anywhere within the spheres of the entire dark universe. The earth was not created as a paradise in the beginning, and it cannot be transformed into one at any point in time. The primordial foundation of the entire universe completely lacks the basic conditions necessary for a true paradise.

Although Jehovah/Allah pretends to reside in heaven, he does not dwell in paradise. In fact, he dwells in a *mystical ghetto*, as images of his throne painted by the prophets of Israel reveal. Mystical nightriders who frequent his so-called heavenly hideout understand exactly what I am saying here. Besides, though he claims to have set the sun in the heavens, he has also "said that he would [continue to] dwell in thick darkness." 1 King 8:12] And a paradise that exists in "thick darkness" is a *mystical ghetto* indeed.

In other words, Jehovah/Allah does not even aspire to ascend to the true Paradise, since he and his occult accomplices have knowingly chosen the path to eternal heirship in the Outer Darkness. The Quran say, "Lo! We [Jehovah/Allah and the so-called archangels] inherit the earth and all who are thereon, and unto Us they are returned [on the last day]. ... "Lo! and it is We, even We, Who quicken and give death [on earth], and We are the Inheritors [of the treasures of this present darkness]." [Quran 19:40; 15:23]

Darkness is not a harmonious component of a true paradise. True paradise implies absolute happiness, and that cannot exist where absolute goodness does not exist. Absolute goodness means perfection, and that on its part, cannot exist where absolute love is lacking. Genuine love was conspicuously lacking in the foundation of the world. The Garden of Eden, where a slaveholder deployed *"ignorant toilers"* to "till the ground" and to unconditionally worship, praise and pray to him as God, hardly painted the picture of a true paradise.

The Garden of Eden was a human zoo; Jehovah/Allah was a captor and Adam and Eve were his captives. Jerusalem, the present-day Garden of Eden, continues to mirror the horrors of spiritual enslavement. People who have not yet reached this realization are still plagued with Edenic paradise-mentality. In any case, if Jehovah/Allah truly made Eden a paradise in the beginning and he drove Adam and Eve away from it when they disobeyed him, then the Garden of Eden ought to still exist as a paradise to this day.

According to the Torah, Jehovah/Allah returned Abram to the same mock paradise of Eden when he abducted him from the city of Ur. But well-documented evidence shows that Abraham did not return to a paradise but to a region of the earth that lacked even drinking water and other staple necessities of decent existence. The

Jewish Exodus that returned to the same so-called "Promised Land" did not also experience a paradise. They were rather tormented, slaughtered and eventually expelled from there just as Adam and Eve were.

Present-day Israelis, once again, returned and presently dwell in the New Eden and it has been far from a paradise to them. In fact, Jehovah/Allah's Garden of Eden has never been a paradise, but "a place that devours its inhabitants." Historical facts speak for themselves.

During the separation of Lot and Abram, Lot had compared Jehovah/Allah's paradise of Eden with the well-watered valley of Jordan, and with the land of Egypt. Genesis 13:10 says that "Lot looked up and saw that the whole plain of the Jordan was well watered, like the [Edenic] garden of the Lord, like the land of Egypt." Well, we still have Jordan and Egypt with us today, so we know exactly what Jehovah/Allah's Garden of Eden looked like. Certainly, no honest human being can speak of Jerusalem today as a paradise. No one can imagine that it was ever a paradise or that it will ever become one.

A god that groped in thick darkness in his primordial prison of darkness and afterward continues to dwell in thick darkness in the present world of darkness clearly lacks the wherewithal to have invented a true paradise. But if paradise merely means a "well-watered land" to Jehovah/Allah, then Jordan and Egypt were equally paradise in the beginning.

Jehovah/Allah is simply phony. He knew very well that a true paradise could not possibly exist within the Outer Darkness, so he spent all his time inventing fine excuses to cover his lies and failures. The idea of a *defunct paradise* is just one of the numerous smoke screens invented by Jehovah/Allah's regime of falsehood. The only people that have continued to be fooled by that are religious believers.

The only eternal Paradise in existence is the Father's heavenly Kingdom. As the diagram on page 11 shows, the Father's glorious

Heaven is the realm of eternal Light. It is eternally separated from our present world of darkness, which exists in the Outer Darkness. That is the only place where love and happiness are absolute, where life is perfect and eternally blissful. The Outer Darkness is the direct opposite of the Father's heavenly domain, and it was within that primordial emptiness that our present dark universe was conjured.

Hell, on the other hand, ordinarily means a state or place of extreme pain and anguish. It is not necessarily one fiery, torturous nether place where sinful human beings proceed to after death to be tormented forever for their evil deeds during their earthly life. Hell is the entire universe, which is inhabited by sinful dead spirits outside the Father's realm of perfect existence. Hell is the world as we know it, as it is the dwelling place of sinful dead spirits. Living in sin means living outside the Father's realm of perfect existence and that literally means self-affliction, pains and anguish.

The dwelling place of every perfect spirit is the Father's heavenly Paradise, while the dwelling place of every fallen dead spirit is Hell. As the present dwelling place of all fallen dead spirits, the entire inhabited universe is Hell, not only for humans but also for all projected lifeforms that the fallen spirits have morphed into. Our entire earthly world that represents Jehovah/Allah's theater of wickedness is but a minute sector of the grand universal Hedes. Human beings are fallen, dead spirits; we are all living in hell here on earth. That is equally true for all other lifeforms within all other biospheres, be they animals or extraterrestrials.

Nevertheless, Jesus Christ has made us know that there is an *Interim Paradise*, which is neither within the Father's glorious Kingdom nor within the spheres and jurisdiction of the world. Like the *re-humanization chamber* in the Royal Ship analogy, the *Interim Paradise*, *Interim Haven* or *Transitional Heaven* is the blessed sanctuary for all the spirits that are already redeemed out of the world. It is specifically set up and overseen by Jesus Christ, who is our sole Messiah or Rescue Officer.

The *Interim Paradise* is not a place where *good* human beings go to when they die to "**behold the glorious presence of the Father**," as customary Christianity insinuates. It is the place where **spirits that have received the salvation of Jesus Christ** proceed to after physical death in the world. All the redeemed spirits must wait here in safety, comfort and harmony with divine ideals until the ultimate resurrection day when the Messiah would officially present them before the Father in his heavenly Paradise.

It is important to note that the heavenly Paradise is not necessarily for *good* human beings, but for all repentant spirits that receive the salvation of Jesus Christ. Jesus Christ does not count us as good or evil the way humans do. Although he was the "Good Shepherd" himself, he even said to people who called him "Good Teacher," "Why do you call me good? No one is good but the Father alone." [Mark 10:18] Indeed, he came into the world not necessarily to save good people, but evil and sinful spirits.

No one is good in the world because the world itself is a sinful creation. That is why the Psalmist said that "we were brought forth in iniquity, and in sin did our mothers conceive us." [Psalms 51:5] I recall the case of the thief that was nailed at the right-hand side of Jesus Christ at Calvary. He did not die a *good* man, but he miraculously recognized and received the salvation of his only Savior, even at his dying moment. That earned him automatic transition into the *Interim Paradise*. The Messiah confirmed that by saying to him, "Truly, I say to you, today you will be with me in Paradise." [Luke 23:43]

Indeed, though Jehovah/Allah reckoned Abraham as "righteous," he still would not have made it to the *Interim Paradise* if he did not eventually recognize and 'see the day of the salvation of Jesus Christ.' Even though his true name was "Abram," meaning *"the Father is exalted,"* he would have remained doomed as a *favored slave* of Jehovah/Allah. But Jesus Christ confirmed to his Jewish followers that Abraham was indeed saved. He said to them, "Your father Abraham rejoiced that he was to see my day; he saw it and was glad [to have made it to the *Interim Paradise*]." [John 8:56]

I should reiterate therefore, that the so-called heaven that blind mystics shuttle daily while still wearing human cloaks on earth is neither the *Interim Paradise* nor the true heavenly Paradise. It was evident that even Paul, as the official founder of customary Christianity, was a blind mystic himself. It was not surprising that he was a principal exponent of this paradisiacal mirage. He cryptically spoke of his personal journey into Paradise this way: "I know a man in Christ who fourteen years ago was **caught up to the third heaven**—whether in the body or out of the body I do not know, God knows. And I know that this man was caught up into Paradise—whether in the body or out of the body I do not know, God knows—and **he heard things that cannot be told, which man may not utter.**" [2 Cor 12:2-4]

The questions that people should ask here are:
- Why was that man's mystical experience of being 'caught up into Paradise' so important to Paul that he had to make it a part of the Scripture?
- How did Paul know everything about this man's so-called ascent, but not whether he was really caught up 'in the body or out of the body'?
- What could the man have heard in the so-called paradise that he could not utter, when Jesus Christ has enjoined his true disciples to reveal every truth they hear without fear or bias? "What I tell you in the dark, utter in the light; and what you hear whispered, proclaim upon the housetops," he says to them. [Matthew 10:27]

Of course, Paul was indirectly speaking about his own personal mystical experience during his Arabian Desert tutorial. In any case, *God knows* that there is an unbridgeable chasm between the Father's true Paradise and every sphere of the world. No human being can ever be caught up into the true Paradise, "whether in the body or out of the body." None can ever listen to the discussions of perfect spirits in the Father's Heaven or of the redeemed spirits in the Interim Paradise. Most certainly, no one who ascends to the true Paradise can possibly come back to any sphere of the world. So, Paul clearly gave himself out here as a fake apostle of Jesus Christ.

If Paul or his mysterious friend had really gone to the Father's true Paradise, or to the Interim Paradise, they would not have been able to say so to any human being on earth. The Interim Paradise is the Muster Station for spirits that are already cleared from the world. None returns to the world from there because that would only mean spiritual retrogression, much like stepping back into spiritual death.

Jesus Christ emphasized this fact with the parable of "Lazarus and the Rich Man." Lazarus and Abraham were in the Interim Paradise, while the Rich Man was still in the hellish world and asking them for water to quench his thirst. According to the narrative, "Abraham said [to the Rich Man], 'Son ... **between us and you a great chasm has been fixed**, in order that those who would pass from here to you may not be able, and none may cross from there to us.'" [Luke 16:25-26]

To fully appreciate the true meaning of the Interim Paradise, it would be helpful for people to know that it is strictly an aspect of the redemptive mission of Jesus Christ. It would also be helpful to revert to the diagram on page 11, and to the Royal Ship analogy. As the diagram shows, the Interim Paradise is an intermediate glorious abode beyond the actual Kingdom of the Father and outside the physical and mystical spheres of the world.

Much like the re-humanization chamber in the Royal Ship analogy, set up by the longsuffering Chief Officer for the purpose of assembling and rehabilitating repentant fish-humans, the Interim Paradise is a sort of *re-spiritualization chamber* for redeemed spirits, overseen exclusively by Jesus Christ, the Master of our salvation race. Therefore, the Interim Paradise is not only where redeemed spirits wait for the ultimate resurrection day, but also where they live the true heavenly lifestyle that is based on true love.

For a fallen dead spirit to qualify for ascent into the Interim Paradise, he must possess knowledge of the truth, accept Jesus Christ as his personal Savior and embrace the heavenly lifestyle, which Jesus Christ epitomizes. Every spirit that truly receives Jesus Christ in the world will automatically re-identify himself with his proper spiritual heritage in absolute goodness. His name will automatically appear in the Interim Paradise.

Such a spirit will not need to become perfect in the sinful world before he is accepted because that is practically impossible. Jesus Christ will become his perfection, and he says, "Truly, truly, I say to you, he who believes has eternal life." The Scripture further says, "To all who received him [Jesus Christ], who believe in his name, he gave power to become children of the Father; who were born, not of blood nor of the will of the flesh, nor of the will of man, but of the Father." [John 6:47;1:12-13]

People can also try to appreciate the true meaning of the Interim Paradise in terms of the *decompression chamber* in which underwater divers are immediately rehabilitated after a prolonged deep underwater operation. Underwater divers breathing compressed air are particularly susceptible to a form of decompression sickness known as bends—the physiological effects of the formation of gas bobbles in the body due to extreme pressure differences between the varying depths of their working environment and the normal atmospheric pressure.

As the diver descends deeper into the water, the external pressure on him increases proportionally with depth. The compressed air he breathes in is equal in pressure to that of the surrounding water at every depth. The longer he stays down and the deeper he dives, the more compressed gas that is absorbed by his body to balance out the surrounding pressure of the water. When the diver ascends back onboard, he spends some time in a controlled environment for the additional gases to leave his body slowly or they will form bobbles in his body tissues.

Therefore, the *decompression chamber* is where deep sea divers are literally helped to return to being normal human beings. Likewise, redeemed spirits literally transit into perfect spirits beings in the Interim Paradise, pending the ultimate return to the actual heavenly Paradise. Every aspect of life in the Interim Paradise is glorious and in strict accordance with the heavenly norm. The redeemed spirits dwell in perfection there, but a chasm still separates them from the presence of the Father.

JESUS CHRIST IS THE SOLE CUSTODIAN OF THE INTERIM PARADISE

The Interim Paradise is strictly a principal feature of the third phase of Christ's redemptive mission in the world. Like the longsuffering Chief Officer in the Royal Ship analogy, Jesus Christ is the Supreme Custodian of the Interim Paradise because he is the Father's sole Rescue Officer to the world. No one is like him in the entire inhabited universe.

The Scripture says that "the Father so loved the world that he gave [sent] his **only** Son, that whoever believes in him should not perish but have eternal life." [John 3:16] And it goes ahead to say, "Therefore the Father has highly exalted him and bestowed on him the name which is above every name [whether of gods or men ever known and worshiped in the world], that at the name of Jesus [Christ not Jehovah/Allah] every knee should bow, in heaven[s] and on earth and under the earth, and every tongue confess that **Jesus Christ [not Jehovah/Allah] is Lord, to the glory of the Father**." [Philippians 2:9-11]

What this means is that the Father endowed Jesus Christ with full autonomy in all aspects of his redemptive mission in the world. He is the autonomous Messiah and Master of our salvation race. No other name or entity deputizes for him. Neither Jehovah/Allah nor the so-called archangels of this world of darkness have a place in the divine mission of Jesus Christ, except in their capacities as obstacles that true seekers of spiritual salvation must overcome to attain rebirth.

That is why only Jesus Christ can authoritatively make these self-proclamations:

- "I am the [only] Son of God."   [John 10:36]

- "I am from Above."   [John 8:23]

- "I am the Living Bread which came down from Heaven."   [John 6:51]

- "I am the Light of the World."   [John 9:5]

- I am the Bread of Life."   [John 6:35]

- "I am the True Vine."   [John 15:1]

- "I am the Good Shepherd."   [John 10:11]

- "I am the Door of the [Lost] Sheep."   [John 10:9]

- "I am the Way, and the Truth, and the Life."   [John 14:6]

- "I am the Resurrection and the Life."   [John 11:25]

Some customary Christians misconstrue these unique designations and refer to Jesus Christ as the "King of kings." This is completely inapplicable. The redemptive mission of Jesus Christ in the world has absolutely nothing to do with kingship of any kind. In fact, when Pontius Pilate asked him, "So you are a king?" He replied, "**You say that I am a king**." Then he added, "For this [only] I was born, and for this [only] I have come into the world, **to bear witness to the truth**." [John 18:36-37]

Jesus Christ came into the world to inform and to rekindle fallen dead spirits and not to become king over them. His unique divine position should not be confused with that of Jehovah/Allah whose chronic obsession has always been to become king over all humans and kings on the earth.

The "King of kings and Lord of lords" spoken off in Revelation 19:11-16 has absolutely no likeness with Jesus Christ our Messiah and the Prince of Peace. Certainly, Jesus Christ is not the mysterious entity in the passage; whose "*eyes are like a flame of fire,*" who "*is clad in a robe dipped in blood,*" who "*will rule them [humankind] with a rod of iron,*" and who "*will tread the wine press of **the fury of the wrath** of God the Almighty.*" Clearly, the wordings do not apply to Jesus Christ:

> "Then I saw heaven opened, and behold, a white horse! He who sat upon it is called Faithful and True, and in righteousness he judges and makes war. **His eyes are like a flame of fire**, and on his head are many diadems; and he has a name inscribed which no one knows but himself. **He is clad in a robe dipped in blood**, and the name by which he is called is The Word of God. And the armies of heaven, arrayed in fine linen, white and pure, followed him on white horses. From his mouth issues a sharp sword with which to smite the nations, and **he will rule them with a rod of iron; he will tread the wine press of the fury of the wrath of God the Almighty. On his robe and on his thigh he has a**

name inscribed, King of kings and Lord of lords." [Revelation 19:11-16]

So-called born-again Christians who clamor about *the rapture* and about their imaginary election as *co-rulers* with Jesus Christ in his kingdom are equally mistaken. It is obvious that they do not quite understand the true nature of the divine mission of the Messiah. Instead of approaching the issue of spiritual salvation as fallen, dead, prodigal spirits who are no longer worthy of being called sons of the Father, they ignorantly brag and exalt themselves as would-be co-rulers in Christ's heavenly kingdom. Notwithstanding that Jesus Christ plainly tells them that he has come into the world in search of *sinners*.

For fallen dead spirits in the world, aspiring to rule over perfect living spirits in the heavenly Kingdom of the Father is the worst symptom of spiritual lostness. True disciples of Jesus Christ know that Jesus Christ did not come into the world to recruit co-rulers for his heavenly kingdom. He came to resurrect spirits that are already self-condemned to eternal death. So, just like the proverbial prodigal sons, they are permanently humbled by the Father's gracious offer of an undeserved second chance. They are genuinely meek and gentle, and they earnestly pray to be readmitted even as the least in the perfect heavenly Kingdom of the Father.

The Scripture makes it clear in John 3:16 that "the Father so loved the world that he gave [sent] his only Son, that whoever believes in him should not perish but have [re-again] eternal life," and not that they should become co-rulers of any kind. Jesus Christ himself, says clearly that he came to seek and save lost sinful spirits, "I came not to call the righteous, but sinners. ... "For the Son of man came to seek and to save the lost. ... [So], "Truly, truly, I say to you, whoever does not receive the kingdom of the Father like a [lost sinful] child shall not enter it." [Matthew 9:6; Luke 19:10; 18:17]

Indeed, judging from our worldly title-mentality, the Interim Paradise is literally the "personal kingdom" of Jesus Christ, since the Father had made him the sole custodian of it by virtue of his exclusive charge over his entire redemptive mission. It can also be argued that when he said to Pontius Pilate, "My kingship is not of this world," it was understood that he was, indeed, a king somewhere. Nevertheless, Jesus Christ never thought of or carried himself as a king in the world. That was not the theme of his divine mission in the world at all.

The following Scriptural verses completely capture the official attitude or position of Jesus Christ on the worldly concept of kingship or rulership:

- "You know that the rulers of the Gentiles lord it over them, and their great men exercise authority over them. It shall not be so among you; but whoever would be great among you must be your servant, and whoever would be first among you must be your slave; **even as the Son of man came not to be served but to serve**, and to give his life as a ransom for many." [Matthew 20:25-28]

- Jesus Christ may be regarded as the "Spiritual King" of the Interim Paradise, yet the Scripture says, "though he was in the form of the Father, [he] did not count equality with the Father a thing to be grasped, but [he] emptied himself, taking the form of a servant, being born in the likeness of men. And being found in human form he humbled himself and became obedient unto death, even death on a cross [that he may become our exemplar]." [Philippians 2:6-8]

By his exemplary life on earth, he showed his true disciples that salvation is not really about *kingship* and *rulership*, but strictly about genuine repentance and humility. "Blessed are the poor in spirit, for theirs is the kingdom of heaven," he says. ... "Take my yoke upon you and learn from me; for I am gentle and lowly in heart, and you will find rest for your spirits. ... "He who is greatest among you shall be your servant; whoever exalts himself will be humbled, and whoever humbles himself will be exalted [into the Interim Paradise]." [Matthew 5:3; 11:29; 23:11-12]

Even then, the Interim Paradise is strictly a transitory kind of kingdom. At the conclusion of his divine mission of salvation, Jesus Christ would officially resurrect and escort all the redeemed spirits there back to the only actual eternal Kingdom of the Father. 1 Corinthians 15:27-28 explain the same fact this way:

"'For the Father has put all things in subjection under his feet.' But when it says, 'All things are put in subjection under him,' it is plain that he is excepted who put all things under him. When all things are subjected to him, then the Son himself will also be subjected to him who put all things under him, that the Father may be everything to everyone [in his eternal heavenly Paradise]."

On the last day, the Father's grace and glory would be withdrawn from every sphere of the Outer Darkness, and the Interim Paradise as presently constituted would be no more. All that would exist, once more, would be the one harmonious household of living spirits in the Father's heavenly Paradise and the band of unrepentant dead spirits remaining self-condemned in the Outer Darkness. As the Scripture says, "they [the unrepentant] will go away into eternal [self-]punishment, but the righteous into eternal life." [Matthew 25:46]

THE ULTIMATE RESURRECTION

The Day of Resurrection will mark the ultimate fulfillment of the Father's Divine Will or Word of Life for the world. As we all know, everything that has a beginning must also have an end. The Father's Word of Life first appeared as the Spirit of Knowledge in

Eden at the *beginning* of the Father's redemptive mission in the world. He later incarnated as Jesus Christ of Nazareth in Jerusalem, the *new* Eden. He would fully accomplish his mission and return to the Father on the Day of Resurrection. On that day, the Messiah would officially restore the redeemed spirits back to their full spiritual selfhood. Most importantly, he would finally return them to their proper dwelling place in the heavenly household of the Father in his eternal glorious Kingdom.

The Father sent the Son into the nether world to redeem and restore all repentant fallen dead spirits to their spiritual glory. The Great Day of Resurrection is what the Scripture simply refers to as the "Great Day of Judgment" in which Jesus Christ will finally separate the saved from the eternally self-condemned, "the wheat from the weed." That day will represent the official close of the Father's grace upon the world and signify the official end of the mission of Jesus Christ, the Father's Word of Life, in the world.

The Scripture explains the end as the final gathering of all peoples of the world before the Messiah for the ultimate separation of the sons of resurrection from the sons of eternal perdition. It says, "Before him will be gathered all the nations, and he will separate them one from another as a shepherd separates the sheep from the goats, and he will place the sheep at his right hand, but the goats at the left. Then the King will say to those at his right hand, 'Come, O blessed of my Father, inherit the kingdom prepared for you from the foundation of the world;' ... Then he will say to those at his left hand, 'Depart from me, you cursed, into the eternal fire prepared for [Jehovah/Allah] the devil and his angels;' ... And they will go away into eternal [self-]punishment, **but the righteous into eternal life**." [Matthew 25:32-34, 41, 46]

It should be stressed that Christ's Final Judgment on the world has absolutely nothing to do with Jehovah/Allah's Armageddon-type Last Judgment of wrath and indignation that would be characterized by "blood and fire and columns of smoke." [Joel 2:30] Jesus Christ simply says, "If anyone hears my sayings and does not keep them, I do not judge him; for I did not come to judge the world but to save the world. He who rejects me and does not receive my sayings has a judge; the word that I have spoken will be his judge on the last day. ... "And this is [will be] the judgment, that the Light has come into the world, and men loved darkness rather than light, because their deeds were evil." [John 12:47-48; 3:19]

CONCLUSION

Jesus Christ did not come into the world to judge, scare or bully anyone into accepting the Father's divine amnesty and offer of spiritual restoration. He came to tell us the truth about who we were and who we have become. He came to help us to appreciate the difference between our lost heavenly life of perfection and the life of spiritual bondage and death that we live now in the Outer Darkness, so that people might freely choose between the two. He is our heavenly Restore Guide.

The way of Jesus Christ is **the way of truth and eternal life,** while the way of Jehovah/Allah is **the way of falsehood, fear and eternal death**. Every time that Jesus Christ stressed the need for people to repent and be born anew, he never said or implied in any way, that the Father would torment anyone who fails to receive his offer of eternal life. What he said repeatedly throughout his earthly ministry was that people who refuse to repent and be born anew would not experience the glory of the Father within them now, and on the last day, would not be counted worthy to attain ultimate spiritual resurrection.

Operatives of worldly religions preach a certain dreadful Day of Judgement when Jehovah/Allah would cast people who do not believe in him into hell fire and torment them there forever. This is purely intended to create and sustain irrational fear in religious believers to compel them to surrender their spiritual rights and remain religious slaves of Jehovah/Allah forever. On the contrary, love of the Father drives away all fears and forms an inviolable shield over people who choose Jesus Christ. They experience spiritual rebirth now and are granted the power to become sons of the Father, being the potential *sons of the resurrection*. Jesus Christ assures that "they do not come into any judgement but have passed from death to life."

It depends on every reader therefore, to make the crucial choice now for his own spirit, between fellowship with Jesus Christ, the heavenly Restore Guide, and fellowship with Jehovah/Allah, the Captor and dreadful Foe.

SELECTED BIBLIOGRAPHY

Holy Bible:
Revised Standard Version (RSV).
New Revised Standard Version (NRSV).
Good News Bible – With Deuterocanonical Books/Apocrypha (GNB).
New International Version (NIV).
New World Translation (NWT).
The Meaning of The Glorious Qur'an, Text and Explanatory Translation by Marmaduke Pickthall, Taj Company Ltd.
Holy Qur'an, Translated by M. H. Shakir, Ansariyan Publications, Qum, Islamic Republic of Iran.
John Fowles, "*The Aristos*," Jonathan Cape, London 1965.
Karen Armstrong, "*A History of God*," Ballantine Books, New York, 1994

www.ingramcontent.com/pod-product-compliance
Lightning Source LLC
LaVergne TN
LVHW042249070526
838201LV00089B/82